Fix 'em Up, Rent 'em Out:
How to Start Your Own House Fix-up & Rental Business in Your Spare Time

OR

Create Wealth By Buying, Repairing and Renting Fix-up Houses

Terry Sprouse

D1468282

Planeta Books LLC
Tucson, Arizona

ISBN 978-0-9798566-1-7

This publication is designed to provide accurate and authoritative information in regard to the subject matter covered. It is provided with the understanding that neither the author nor the publisher is engaged in rendering legal, accounting or other professional services. If legal or other expert assistance is required, the services of a competent professional person should be sought.

Published by
Planeta Books LLC
PO Box 41223
Tucson, AZ 85717

For updates and more resources visit:

www.planetabooks.com
www.fixemup.org

Acknowledgements

I would like to thank my wife and fix-up partner Angélica (who thinks she taught me everything I know). She and I together learned the processes discussed in the following pages, and this book would not have been possible without her.

I acknowledge my sons, Jason and Bryan, also active (albeit sometimes unwilling) participants in fix-up projects. I thank my mother, Olive, for her inspiration and encouragement, and my brother, Mike, who has been a constant and unflagging source of assistance in the fix-up process over the years. Mike and I listened to more Sunday morning polka music than is probably healthy, while forging ahead on innumerable repair projects.

Thanks to the ever supportive and always inspiring, Wally Allen, without whose help I could not have gotten started in this business. I acknowledge the insight that I received from Paul Hoyt, someone who refined self-sufficiency to a science, and showed me how to find ways to repair almost anything.

I am grateful to handyman Lee Anderson. He is the best in the business, and has tackled the difficult projects with skill and humor.

I thank Sean McCoy, both an accountant and an educator, who has answered my questions with unerring insight, and has pointed me in the right direction more than once.

I also thank Bob Zachmeier (an outstanding educator, investor, and author), Colleen Filippone, and Robert Merideth. All three offered perceptive comments and suggestions on the draft of this work.

Foreword

When Terry and I first started fixing up houses six years ago, I didn't know the first thing about repairing houses. But it still intrigued me when we found an inexpensive house in a nice neighborhood. Even though the house was a disaster, it seemed like a great opportunity to make some money, and to learn how to make repairs.

I was recently reminded of how far I have come when a friend asked us to look over a house that she was thinking about buying. It was a fix-up in need of repair, but nothing that Terry and I hadn't seen before. We encouraged her to buy it because all of the repairs were within the realm of "doable." For us, it would have been a piece of cake.

I recommend Terry's book to you as a guide on how to get started in the spare-time fix-up business, based on how we did it. And by the way, I taught him everything he knows.

Angy Sprouse

Contents

Introduction

This book is aimed at the person who has a strong desire to invest in real estate but wants to keep his or her regular 9 to 5 job. This person, like me, may not start off with a lot of "disposable income." My wife and I have to pinch pennies and think long and hard before taking the plunge to buy a property. People who do posses the extra money can afford to hire professionals to take much of the burden off their shoulders. They can hire attorneys, real estate agents, landscapers, plumbers and electricians. But for me, the key is not to rely on the so-called real estate professionals. What I propose is that you learn to do all of these things yourself, just as you would learn all aspects of any hobby that you pursue. It is more difficult to do it all yourself, but it is more financially rewarding, more deeply satisfying, and you will learn wide assortment of skills that that will serve you well throughout life.

I encourage you to adopt a new philosophy to go along with your new hobby, one that moves you in the direction of becoming independent and self-reliant.

Components of your new philosophy include:

- Focus your energies on what gives you satisfaction and meaning in life.
- Use problems at work to fuel your desire to succeed in real estate investing.
- Recognize setbacks as opportunities in disguise.
- Absorb new information like a sponge when learning to make your own repairs.
- Don't pay others to do what you can learn to do yourself.
- Make time to learn the necessary skills to earn money

with fix-up houses.

- Have your subconscious "radar" on the look out for fix-up houses that meet your criteria.
- Accept that the only way to learn how to rent out properties, including handling problem tenants, is by doing it.
- Make the repair process a whole family experience.
- Only sell a house in such a way that you pay no federal income taxes.
- Take a steady path to success, learning new skills as you go, gradually building your knowledge and wealth.

This is a slow, steady approach. It doesn't involve buying many houses rapidly, but instead, acquiring properties gradually. Part of the joy of buying a below market priced fix-up house is that you get to repair it. That may take two or three years if you live in the house at the same time, which is one path that I utilize.

My philosophy is that money is not made by buying and selling a lot of houses. I don't have the disposable money to buy a house a year for 10 years. My way to make money in real estate is through careful attention to detail, buying houses in need of repair, adding value to them by fixing them up, renting out the property, managing tenants, and making repairs when tenants leave. I believe in hanging on to what I have and in being self-reliant. My money is made in the trenches, in doing what many people are unwilling to do, or don't feel that the hard work is worth the reward. It involves the drudgery, (for some people, but in reality an opportunity to learn and grow) of cleaning up a house that has been turned inside out by irresponsible tenants.

It also involves dealing with problem tenants who don't pay, or who bother the neighbors, or who don't take care of the house. If you learn to accept, and even enjoy doing the repairs, and learn the proven ways to deal with problem tenants, then you will succeed where most people fail. It all comes down to keeping in view the financial rewards that await you as you learn the necessary skills, and do the inescapable hard work that comes with the hobby. Beyond the financial rewards, there is the satisfaction and confidence that comes with mastering the skills of the profession.

As part of my do-it-yourself philosophy, I have accumulated many books that have been useful. These include volumes on buying real estate, managing real estate, tax guides, business books and technical repair manuals. Throughout the course of this work, I will refer to the books that have been particularly helpful to me, and which will hopefully be useful to you as well. I have made real estate investing my hobby, as have many others, and you can do it too. For anyone who wants to learn there is plenty of room in the fix-up business. Grab a hammer and join me.

1

Focusing Your Energies on What Gives Life Satisfaction and Meaning

I understand now the value of a passion that is never betrayed by insecurity or by defeat or by fear of difficulties.

-Salma Hayek, actress (on directing the movie *Frida*).

Working and Living in Harmony with Your Values

Most people only re-examine the path that their life is taking when they suffer a traumatic experience. Some people reach a point where they realize that their days are numbered. They sense the need to focus the remainder of their lives on doing something that provides a deeper satisfaction and allows them to spend more time with their family. For others, they realize that they don't want to continue to work at a mind-numbing job or for an ungrateful boss.

There is more to life than just making money. Henry David Thoreau said, "Most men live lives of quiet desperation." We long for something more fulfilling.

I advocate investing your time and psychic energy in fix-up houses. You will find more meaning in life, grow as a person, and make money independently of your regular job.

Taking a new path toward earning money requires us "to give up what is familiar and secure," as Marsha Sinetar says in her book *Do What You Love and the Money Will Follow*. Sinetar feels that working at the "right" job involves "doing our best at what we do best." Sinetar suggests that we periodically take stock of our true life's purpose by asking the following questions:

1. What do I want to have accomplished when I look back upon my life in old age?

2. What habits would I need to cultivate and what would I have to delete from my present life to live out my true purpose?

3. What activities would I do if I lived as if my purpose meant something to me?

While you pay a price for following your dream, you also pay a price for staying where you are. You lose the opportunity to develop new life-coping skills that help you deal with unexpected crises or joblessness. You may suffer from depression by staying in a debilitating job. Sinetar, in *To Build the Life You Want, Create the Work You Love,* says that excelling at a job that you love could be the best mental health insurance for people who feel depressed or anxious about their work. Americans spend $12.4 billion each year to treat clinical depression.

Science fiction writer Ray Bradbury, in *Zen and the Art of Writing,* wrote that, "life is short, misery sure, and mortality certain." Yet, he advocated that as we move along life's way, and in our work, our lives should be filled with "zest" and "gusto." With zest and gusto, traveling to the grave, Bradbury vowed to fight injustice, appreciate beauty and encourage children. Is there enough zest and gusto in your life to fight injustice, appreciate beauty and encourage children?

We should wisely use the time that we must devote to work. Our working hours constitute at least one-third of our lives during the work week. As Joe Dominguez and Vicki Robin point out in *Your Money or Your Life,* money is what we chose to trade our time, or "life-energy," for. The authors distinguish between "wants" vs. "needs," and promote not wasting money on unnecessary consumer goods. Instead, they advocate conscientiously saving money until you reach the point where you can free yourself from the working treadmill.

Paul and Sarah Edwards, in *Making It On Your Own,* describe the transformation that takes place when one takes the leap of faith to start a new business, and master it, with this sports analogy.

One day they're struggling to get to the top of their game. They clutch in the clinch. They almost make it. They're inconsistent – brilliant at moments and disappointing at others. And then one day, with dogged determination and after much effort, they do it. They get a perfect ten. They win the title. They break a record. They take the gold medal. And somehow, almost miraculously, at that point they become a champion. They project a new aura of confidence. They begin thinking and walking and talking like a champion.

The independence of working with fix-up houses was this type of "right" job for me, and can be for you too. It can be the road to operate a business that develops one's independence, creativity and imagination. With real estate, you can invest a small amount and gradually accumulate money as both your rents and equity increase over time.

Start by Meandering in the Direction that You Want To Go

If your circumstances are such that it is impossible for you to start investing in real estate today, you can start by just meandering in that direction. You can program your mind to pay attention to anything related to real estate. Cut articles out of the newspaper, buy books at book sales, ask friends and co-workers how they purchased their house, watch for free classes or seminars. You can be constantly learning and preparing for the day you will purchase your first fix-up property. As Paul and Sarah Edwards point out, "virtually anything you need to know is available to you through books, tapes, work-

8

shops, seminars, public education programs, consultants and training programs."

I meandered for approximately 11 years before purchasing my first investment property. Now I wish I had started sooner, but you can't begin until you have the desire and the knowledge. Sometimes, desire and knowledge can be acquired simply by observing someone else operating a successful business.

There are always reasons not to invest in real estate. Most commonly, many people say that house prices are too high, but as Andrew McLean and John Eldred point out in *Investing in Real Estate*, there is a worse time to buy, and that is next year, or in 5 years, or anytime in the future. The best approach says Eldred in *The 106 Common Mistakes Homebuyers Make (and How to Avoid Them)*, is not to wait to buy properties, instead you should buy properties and then wait.

Your Desire Creates the Power to Succeed

Never underestimate the power of sublimation. If you are frustrated enough by your present working situation, you can channel that strong feeling into your new fix-up business. Don't take your anger out on your boss. That would be wasting it. Focus your strong feelings by throwing yourself into repairing your fix up houses. Don't let frustrations at work cause you to be depressed. Instead, use it to fuel the fires. Let it help you start the process of becoming independent, help you move into a more satisfying life.

You should be grateful if you have a boss who constantly rubs you the wrong way. Life may be trying to teach you something. If your boss wasn't such an aggravation, you might never have the motivation to strike out on your own. One of the luckiest days of your life may be when you realize that you could not stand to work for your boss any longer, and you are forced to find a new path.

In the next chapter I will show you why investing your time in fix-up houses is the shortest path to your goals.

2

Why Invest in Fix-up Homes?

Fixing run-down houses is truly a golden opportunity for do-it-yourself real estate investors.

- Jay P. DeCima

Introduction

There are many good reasons to invest in fix-up houses. They provide security in uncertain times, they tend to rise in value faster than most other investments, and you can do it part-time and at almost any age. Fix-up houses have the added advantage of reducing risk by purchasing houses for less money, allowing you to make lower monthly mortgage payments.

Security in Retirement

Are you like me and never socked much away for retirement? You are not alone. The Employee Benefit Research Institute's Annual Retirement Confidence Survey found that pre-retirees (Americans between the ages of 55 and 65) greatly underestimate how long they are likely to live and how much money they will need in retirement.

Experts say that we need to change our mindset from "assets" to "income" in retirement planning. It's not enough to know how much money we have in savings; we need to know how much income our savings can generate over time.

There is no better way to change our mindset and our portfolio from "assets" to "income" than by investing in real estate. If we invest wisely before we retire, and have a stable of reliable rental properties that generate steady monthly income, we can look forward to a retirement that provides security instead of uncertainty.

Security Today

When the shaky economy makes us as nervous as a cat in a room full of rocking chairs, we all want a safe haven for our money. Real estate is at the top of my list of sound investments. Below are five reasons why you can count on real estate to provide you with security today.

Cash flow

With a good rental property, after all the expenses have been covered, including mortgage, vacancy rate, repairs, and property management, you can still receive a good cash flow. This provides a reliable monthly income for as long as you want to keep the property. As the amount of rent that you charge goes up, your profits go up. See Table 2.1 for historic monthly rents in the U.S., from the U.S. Census Bureau.

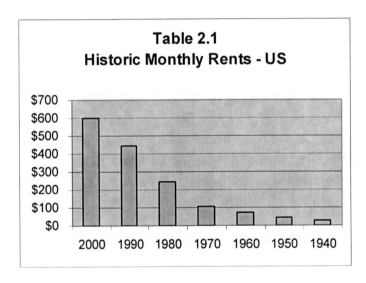

Demand for Housing

With our growing population, a gain of one American born every 14 seconds, we will have a population of 400 million by 2050 compared to today's population of 290 million

(U.S. Census Bureau). With current immigration patterns and population growth, there will continue to be a demand for housing over the next 50 years.

Appreciation

According the U.S. Census Bureau, in 1970 the average value of a house was $65,300. In 2000 the average value had risen to $119,000, an average increase of 3% per year, adjusted for inflation. From 1940 to 2000, the average increase was 5% per year, also adjusted for inflation. Table 2.2 shows historic home values.

To get a true picture of what we can expect to make in house appreciation we have to look at the long-term trends. These trends tell us that we can expect to make between 3% and 5% per year, not counting increases due to inflation. That may seem low, but when we consider that we only put a small percentage down, probably 5-10%, and we receive monthly rent checks that more than cover mortgage payments, it begins to make sense. Periodic housing booms can cause house values to rise dramatically but the trends tell us that we cannot count on these kinds of profits in the long term. However, if history is any indication, we can rely on steady, long-term, profits.

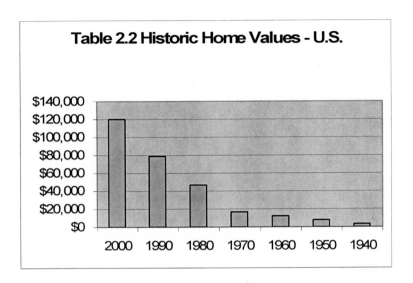

Table 2.2 Historic Home Values - U.S.

Principal pay down

With each mortgage payment, you decrease the amount that you owe on a home loan as you reduce your principal. When your property is rented out, someone else pays your loan for you. Also, equity goes up as property values appreciate over time. Table 2.3 illustrates how the principal of a loan goes down over time at the same time that the house appreciates in value. The original mortgage (loan) is $150,000, which is also the original value of the house. As time goes by, the value of the house increases to $300,000, due to appreciation. At the same time, the amount owed on the mortgage is reduced to $20,000, due to the mortgage being gradually paid down. At this point, the amount of equity (or profit) in the house is $280,000.

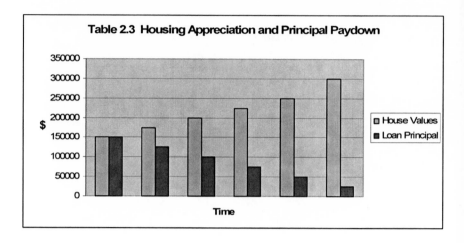

Table 2.3 Housing Appreciation and Principal Paydown

Tax savings

Uncle Sam gives real estate investors tax incentives. The federal government allows you to depreciate your investment (or reduce your taxes to account for physical deterioration of the house) on Schedule E of your annual tax form. In addition, you deduct expenses related to your investment from your gross income on IRS Form 1040, and reduce the amount of income that you pay taxes on.

The Advantage of Real Estate Over Stocks

You are more likely to succeed in real estate than in stocks because you have more control over your real estate investment. As William Nickerson, author of *How I Turned $1,000 into Three Million in Real Estate in My Spare Time*, said, "by comparison (to stocks) you can retain personal control at all stages in the selection, operation and improvement of your income property." When investing in stocks, you relinquish control of your money to a stock manager. Your only decisions are when to buy and sell.

In addition, with real estate you have the potential to realize a much higher return on investment. To purchase stocks you must pay the full price of the stock, and of course, you receive the full benefit when the stock goes up. If you purchase $100,000 of stocks and the value goes up to $150,000, you make $50,000. In real estate, when you take out a loan, you can receive the benefits of the entire value of the real estate by only investing 10%, 5% and sometimes as little as 0%, as a down payment. If you purchase a $100,000 house with $5,000 down, when the value of the house rises to $150,000 you still receive the full $50,000 increase (Table 2.5).

Table 2.5 Returns on Investment Real Estate vs. Stocks (adjusted for inflation)				
	$ Invested	Value	Value in 10 years	Profit
Real Estate	$5,000	$100,000	$150,000	$50,000
Stocks	$100,000	$100,000	$150,000	$50,000

Buying Fix-up Houses Reduces Risk

A fix-up house reduces risk two ways:

1) You pay less money up front and monthly. When you purchase a fix-up house, because it is a house in dire need of repair, you pay a lower price than you would for a house ready for occupancy. By paying a lower price for a house, you pay lower monthly mortgage payments at a time when you will need the extra money to make repairs.

2) You increase your opportunity for profit because you have the built-in profit that can be used as investment

money for the next house that you purchase. You have a built-in financial advantage, because you will increase the value of the house by $20,000-30,000, or more, when you complete the repairs. The value of the house rises to the value of the other houses in the neighborhood.

More Time with Family

Parents want security and safety, and all of the advantages that they themselves didn't have, for their children. Money from real estate can provide that safety cushion. The extra income from real estate allows parents to spend more time with their children and less time working for a company that may not appreciate their efforts. To paraphrase the "golfer's creed," the worst day with your family is better than the best day at the office. When you reach retirement and look back, what really counts is the time spent with family.

You Can Do It Part Time

You don't need to leave a secure job in order to get involved in fix-ups. My fix-up business is my hobby. I do all the work on weekends and evenings. If you have the right perspective on your new hobby, you will look forward to weekends and evenings doing fix-up work, as something fun and exciting.

It's better not to quit your regular job because loan companies like to see regular income, and your job will provide money for fixing up your properties. It's also nice to have your salary as a secure income source for times when unexpected expenses occur, or when you are between tenants.

You Can Start Later (or Earlier) in Life

The U.S. Census Bureau reports that 75 percent of multi-family investors are over the age of 45. Over half of these investors own less than 5 units and they earned roughly 31 percent of their income from their investment properties.

The logic behind these statistics is that most real estate investors come to invest later in life because they are concerned about their retirement and are at their highest potential earning power. Forty-eight percent inherited a home.

While older people tend to build up more financial resources over time, investing in fix-ups is equally suitable for younger people just entering the job market. A young investor could pick up an inexpensive fix-up rental property around a university. In a few years, while he or she is still relatively young, they could make enough money from their real estate properties to have a steady flow of rent money coming in, enough to help pay for a college education.

Women Are Leading the Way

The field of fix-up properties is as open to women as it is to men. As real estate renovator Suzanne Brangham, in *Housewise,* stated, "Having been a wife, a mother, and then a single parent during my fifteen years in this business, I can attest to the fact that this career (of renovating houses) accommodates all life-styles and schedules."

Mary Weir, in her book *House Recycling*, documented how she made $1 million by renovating houses. She learned the necessary repair skills, and she became an expert at repairing mansions. By the end of 15 years she had purchased and repaired 30 houses. Ms. Weir says, "All you need is willingness to learn from books, from professionals, and from trial and error."

Make $106/Day Profit with Just Two Rentals

A relatively small investment in only 2 fix-up properties can generate a good daily profit. Adding together three benefits of owning a rental property illustrates that you can make an additional $106 per day, or $32,000 per year, each day that you hold two rental properties and principal residence (Table 2.6). The components include rental income, principal pay down and increase in equity (not including tax deductions or depreciation.) The value of each house is estimated at $200,000 for a total of $600,000. Granted, you don't see the principal pay down and the increases in equity in a paycheck, yet they still generate wealth behind the scenes that becomes available when you refinance or sell the property.

Table 2.6
Calculating Total Daily Profit

Rent from 2 houses/month (after mortgage payments) $400
Value Increase on $600,000 at 5%/yr = $30,000/yr
divided by 12 for monthly increase $2500
Mortgage pay down (monthly) $300
TOTAL $3200/mo. = $106/day

The next chapter will address the expertise necessary to become an expert in your field.

3
The Rules of the Game: Learn by Doing

Adversity causes some people to break, and other people to break records.

Learn the Ropes

My wife and I didn't know much about repairing houses before we started the fix-up business, but like fine wine, we got better as time went on. One important rule in the fix-up profession is that you must constantly strive to become self-sufficient and learn all aspects of the profession. You must become an expert in your new profession/hobby. You can learn from others, but you have to rely on yourself to get ahead. Like the novice swimmer who is tossed in the pool, sometimes it is sink or swim. You must learn by doing.

Trust Your Own Judgment

There are times when destiny forces you down a certain path in life. Other times, you make you own destiny by forcing yourself down a path.

My plan when I bought my first fix-up house was to learn by doing. I thought if others had learned to do it, so could I. When you buy your fist fix-up house, it is like being stranded on a desert island. You are forced to learn new skills to survive. Perhaps the best way to learn new skills is by putting yourself in a situation where you are forced to change and adapt. As the hero was told in the book *Dune*, "Unless you change, something inside you sleeps."

To speed up the learning processes, you need to have a collection of reference books on home repair, buying and selling houses, rental properties, tax law and all other aspects of real estate. If a home without books is like a body without a soul, then a fix-up business without reference books is like a cook without a cookbook.

You may not know everything at the start of your new business and you may need help in some areas, especially in the initial stages. However, each time you pay to have someone do work for you, or go through some new process, you should observe everything, ask questions and learn the process. This way, the next time you will be able to do it yourself, or at least perform a larger part of it. The key is to keep doing things over and over until you master how it works. You will eventually reach a point where you make decisions of where to make repairs and which houses to buy based on your instinct.

Learn to Make Repairs

Never miss an opportunity to do your own repair work. Think of it as part of your educational process. You lose two ways when you hire someone to do your work. First, you lose the chance of a free education, and second you lose the money that you would have saved by doing it yourself. It may take you four hours to change an electrical receptacle or fix a toilet that won't flush, something a professional could do in minutes. Don't be concerned, in the long run you have learned a skill to be used for the rest of your life. More on this topic in Chapter 6.

After going through my explanation about how everyone can learn to repair a house, a friend of mine insisted that it was impossible for him to do fix-up work; it just wasn't in his genes. I replied that his way of thinking was his dogma. My karma told me that he could do it. In time, little by little, he did learn to make repairs and he came to enjoy it, even relish it. My karma ran over his dogma.

Having said the above, I also think that you should have a good handyman to back you up. Although there are many things that you can learn to do, you also have to know your limitations. There will be times when you can't make a complicated repair. Someone with experience must be called in. For many things you can be the expert, but for some things you can't. Ideally you should establish a good working relationship with a true handyman that you trust and is available to help you out as needed, particularly in the first few years of your business.

Learn to Buy, Rent and Pay Taxes

Other topics for you to master include how to buy and sell a house, managing rental property, and taxes. Again, you must strive to become an expert. No one will ever work as hard for you as you will work for yourself. However, there is a lot to learn from real estate agents who are involved in investing. Talking to other investors who do the same thing that you do is a great way of sharing information and learning from each other. If the community college offers a class by a real estate agent who knows investing, take the course. I have taken courses from real estate agents who teach just such classes through community colleges and open universities. The meager cost of the course is far outweighed by the benefits you receive. I first learned how to take the cash out of one house by refinancing to buy the next house at a community college course. Sit in the front row and ask a lot of questions, you will probably get some good answers. A good question is the beginning of wisdom.

While it may be useful to utilize a real estate agent when buying a house, I don't usually use an agent to sell a house. I generally don't recommend selling a house as it has long-term value as a rental. However, sometimes you are in a situation where it makes sense to sell a house, such as when taking advantage of the Tax Payer Relief Act exemption (discussed in Chapter 7). Your attitude should be that you want to learn how to do it yourself. You don't learn to ride a bike by watching someone else do it. The only way to learn is by doing it yourself, and the more you do it, the better you will be at it. Besides making more money, your attitude is that you want to practice doing all the steps in the process of selling until it becomes second nature for you.

An "expert" may have more experience than you or I do, but experience does not make up for commitment. They may be involved in the process, but you are committed. It's like the difference between the chicken and the pig in a ham and egg breakfast. The chicken is involved but the pig is committed.

Always Get Two Bids and Make Lots of Calls

No matter what you do in your fix-up business, if it involves spending money, always get at least two bids. This applies not only to large jobs you will have to contract out, but also, and especially when you are applying for a mortgage. If someone knows that you are only getting one bid, they will charge you more. It doesn't matter if they say they are a discount company, if they say they are giving you the best deal possible, if they say they like to help out the little guy just getting started in a fix-up business. It is a law of nature that you will pay more.

I had a student in one of my classes who said that she always used the same mortgage company for loans, and the company always gave her a good deal. My response was that of the two statements she had just made, only one of them could be true. I asked her how she could ever know if she was getting a good deal if she didn't get good faith estimates (or GFE, an estimate of your settlement costs and loan terms) from at least two different companies. She said that she trusted her loan agent. Maybe she was getting a good deal, but she would never know if she was or not, unless she got another GFE from another company. It is a simple matter to just call another company and have them fax, or email you, a good faith estimate. My experience has been that there is a huge reduction in the price that you pay for a mortgage when you get two estimates, especially when you are just starting your fix-up business.

The two-bid rule also applies when hiring outside help. The first investment house I bought had eight windows that were broken on the back and side of the house, two of which were sliding glass doors. It looked like it was going to cost me a tidy sum to get them fixed. I requested bids from five companies. Some bids came back as high as $500, and none less than $300. The 7th company I called said he could do the job for $175 dollars. The owner of the company was a one-man operation who did all the work himself, and did it well. Persistence paid off. Yet now, if I were faced a similar situation of eight broken windows, I would save even more money by replacing them myself.

How I Do My Calculations

The one key question that you must answer before you purchase a property is, "am I going to make money on my fix-up house?" If you do the calculations and find that you are going to be losing money each month, look for another house. You won't be in this business very long if you can't show a positive cash flow each month.

There are three calculations you must do in order to make an informed choice about buying a house (Table 3.1):

1. Determine the monthly mortgage payments that you

will be making, including principal, interest, taxes and insurance (PITI).

2. How much rent can you expect to receive each month.
3. Subtract calculation 1 from calculation 2.

Table 3.1
Calculating Cash Flow

1. Sales Price   _____
2. Down Payment   _____
3. Amount of Mortgage (1 minus 2)   _____
4. Interest Rate   _____
5. Monthly Principal & Interest (P&I)   _____
6. Taxes & Insurance (T&I)   _____
7. PITI (5+6)   _____
8. Rental payments to you   _____
9. Monthly profit   _____

To calculate the amount of principal and interest that you pay each month refer to Table 3.2. If you are taking out a $100,000 mortgage for 30 years at 6% mortgage rate, multiply 100 X $6.00 = $600 P&I (principal and interest) per month. You must add monthly taxes and insurance (T&I) charges to get the entire monthly payment. You can find the taxes either from the county courthouse or, more simply, looking at the taxes that other houses in the neighborhood pay. The taxes are also listed on the flyers that real estate agents hand out at the houses or by checking the multiple listing service (MLS) online for other houses that are being sold in the neighborhood. Insurance can be found the same way. I assume that the tenant will pay all of the utilities so I don't include those in the monthly calculations.

To calculate how much you can expect to rent the

27

house for is equally as simple. Call all the houses that have "for rent" signs in their front yard. Ideally, if you have done your homework and kept track of what houses are renting for prior to deciding to buy, you will already know the rents. I suggest that you keep a list with the property addresses in one column and the amount of rent in a second column. Or, you can do it the fast way and just place the "for rent" flyers in a file folder each time you find one.

Table 3.2
Monthly Cost of Principal and Interest for 30-Year Loan per $1,000 of mortgage

Multiply the cost per $1,000 by the size of the mortgage (in thousands). The result is the monthly payment for principal and interest (P&I).
For example, for a $100,000 mortgage for 30 years at 6 % mortgage rate (MR) multiply 100 x $6.00 = $600 P&I per month.

MR	P & I	MR	P&I	MR	P&I
5.00%	$5.37	6.50%	$6.32	8.375%	$7.43
5.125	5.44	6.875	6.57	8.500	7.52
5.250	5.52	7.000	6.66	8.375	7.61
5.375	5.60	7.125	6.74	8.500	7.78
5.500	5.69	7.250	6.83	8.625	7.87
5.625	5.76	7.375	6.91	8.750	7.06
5.750	5.84	7.500	7.00	8.875	8.05
6.000	6.00	7.625	7.08	9.375	8.41
6.125	6.08	7.875	7.17	9.500	8.50
6.250	6.15	8.000	7.26	9.625	8.60
6.375	6.24	8.125	7.34	9.875	8.69
				10.00	8.78

After subtracting the PITI from you monthly rents, you should have a rough idea of how much you will make each month. In general, you should try to make a minimum each month of $100, although I admit that I've gone lower. On my first rental property, rents were the same as the mortgage payments, so I was only breaking even. However, it is best if you can allow for some margin of error. It is normal that property taxes and house insurance goes up over time, and those will quickly eat into your profits. More is always better when it comes to monthly profit from rents, so if you can get $200 per month you are much better off. If you aren't turning at least a small profit each month, you may need to take a different approach. One way is to increase the size of your down payment to the point where you do show a profit. A second way is to negotiate a lower price on the house, or look for another house that needs more fix-up work and is priced cheaper.

A quick rule of thumb is that for each $100,000 you pay on a mortgage, you need to receive about 1% of that amount (or $1,000 in rent) in order to pay the mortgage. The 1% rule lets you quickly decide which properties are worth considering and which you should not bother with.

Do the Math - Don't Leave Your Profits to Chance

You must be absolutely clear in your own mind that the property you buy will make money for you. No one else can tell you this. You must practice "running the numbers" or using your calculator to add up all of the costs associated with a purchase and then calculate what you stand to make. Stay up all night if you need to, to make sure the numbers work for you prior to purchasing any house. Do the calculation over and over until it makes sense to you. Practice running the numbers on each house you see, regardless of whether or not you plan to buy the house. After some practice, you will be able to run the numbers in your mind, and have a good idea of whether or not the house is worth pursuing.

4

The Nuts and Bolts of Buying Fix-up Houses

I will prepare myself and perhaps my chance will come.

-Abraham Lincoln

The Foundation

There is no substitute for planning carefully before buying your first fix-up property. The more information that you gather before you buy, the better the probability that you will buy a good investment house. The two foundational criteria that I look for in making any decision to purchase an investment property are:

1. The house is either in a nice, or a mixed, neighborhood.
2. The house is in need of fix-up.

The Target Neighborhood: Nice and Not-So-Nice Houses

One target neighborhood is in an area where you are reasonably certain that property values will increase over time. This type of neighborhood is fairly easy to spot as you can see that home owners are taking good care of their homes, with the exception of the one that you are buying. You can look for flowers in front yards, nice landscaping, recently painted houses, and nice neighborhood parks. These are the types of neighborhood that should be your target area. If you want to see what a neighborhood is really like, drive by at night and see how many people are walking around the neighborhood. If people walk around the streets at night and there is low automobile traffic that's a good sign. Things to watch out for in the neighborhood on the negative side are cars parked on front yards, too many cars parked around a house, junk in front or back yards, worn out roofs or houses in serious need of repair. The ideal location is where most of the people living in the neighborhood own their homes and there are only a few rentals. Rentals tend not to be cared for as well as homes that are occupied by the owners.

Buy houses that are 3-4 bedrooms and 2 baths, something with enough room that the average American family would want to live there. After you fix up the house you will need to be able to rent it out, so you want something that has the broadest possible appeal. Unless you focus on a specialized rental group, like university students, if the house is too small you will get people who won't stay very long.

Although in this type of neighborhood property values are likely to increase more rapidly than other areas, you pay more to buy a house here, and the rent payments are not much different from what you get in a not-so-nice neighborhoods. That is why I also recommend houses in mixed, or lower priced, areas of town.

Mixed neighborhoods, where there are both nice houses and not-so-nice houses offer the advantage of buying properties that you pay less for, yet you can still charge about the same rent as you charge in nicer areas, giving you more profit. These neighborhoods are not as nice as some neighborhoods, but not completely run down either. Property values are generally lower. You will buy these kinds of houses to provide you with the monthly income you need to keep your business going. You should try to get houses both in nice neighborhoods and in mixed neighborhoods.

Table 4.1 compares profits for two of my rental houses from two different areas of town. The Richey Street property is near a central part of town where property values are lower. The Planeta Avenue property is in a nicer area on the edge of town where new growth is taking place.

	Mortgage	Rent	Profit	Present Value
Table 4.1 **Rental Profits**				
Richey Street	$504	$715	$211	$130,000
Planeta Ave.	$703	$875	$172	$185,000

Jay DeCima, author of *Investing in Fixer-Uppers*, likes to invest in the older residential sections of a city that surround the downtown area. He has found that these are the best locations to buy for cash flow. DeCima states that "Renters are willing to pay top dollar (for these older properties), because they're close to shopping, yet still able to enjoy the privacy of residential neighborhoods."

Finding Housing Information

There are many cheap and effective ways to learn important information on housing prices and conditions in your target area. My wife and I pick up house-for-sale flyers from the for sale houses in target areas and we go to all open houses. In Sunday's newspaper is also a listing of all houses sold for each week and the price, broken down by zip code. We are avid readers of the newspaper house-for-sale want ads in the real estate section.

Look on the internet, under county statistics to find out what a house last sold for, or to use the MLS. For a free, instant valuation of a property I have used zillow.com. The website provides a valuation of the house, aerial photos of the property, and other useful information. It can be found at:

http://www.zillow.com/

Selecting Fix-up Houses

In identifying a fix-up house, you want one that is about $20-30,000 less than what it might sell for, if you sold it after fixing it up. This means that prior to buying this property you must do a comparative analysis of other houses that have sold in this neighborhood that are similar to the one you want to buy. You can do this most easily by asking the agent selling the house to provide you with a list of houses that have sold in the last six months in that area. If the agent is prepared, he will already have a list ready to hand out. The goal of your market analysis is to find houses that are exactly like the one you are looking at and to see what they sold for. Make sure that you compare apples to apples, and compare houses with the same square footage, number of rooms and bathrooms, air conditioning, garage or carport and other characteristics. Calculate an average price that houses similar to yours sold for. Then subtract the amount you would pay for the house, to determine the amount of equity you would have. Equity is the amount of money you would receive after fixing up and selling the house (or, re-financing the house).

Equity should increase over time if you bought your house in a neighborhood where houses consistently increase in value. However we are not counting on that. The only thing we count on is that there is equity in the house when we buy it. Another cost you will face, in addition to fix-up costs, are closing costs which are usually around 3% every time you buy or sell a house. That's why we need a good chunk of equity in the house to begin with, to cover closing costs, fix-up costs and to have some money left over for future investments.

Chance Favors the Prepared Mind

Because a fix-up house will be your bread and butter, and because you won't be the only one looking for them, you must be prepared to act quickly once a target property is first put on the market. You'll want to identify target neighborhoods where you would like to invest, as well as identify unwanted neighborhoods where you would never invest. You must do your homework thoroughly. You have to know what houses sell for in your target neighborhoods, so that you can recognize a bargain property when it appears. If it's your first house, you should be pre-qualified for a loan (so you know what size loan you qualify for). Then you must be able to size up the neighborhood and quickly purchase the house before someone else gets it before you.

Don't get too discouraged if you don't land the first few houses that you try to purchase. Fix-up houses are like taxi cabs. If you miss one, there will always be another one coming.

Key Advantages of Fix-ups

The three great advantages of buying fix-up houses are:

1.) You buy them for much less than you would pay for a normal house, so you spend less of your investment money to get in;

2.) Because the price is less, monthly mortgage payments are also lower than if you had bought a traditional house;

3.) After the repairs are completed, the house automatically increases in value, and is valued the same as other houses in the neighborhood. This is a faster and more certain way to add value, rather than having to wait for housing prices to appreciate. See Table 4.2 for how appreciation takes place over a two-year period.

Table 4.2 Calculating Equity for a Fix-up House	
Purchase Price	$200,000
Value After Repairs (20% increase)	$240,000
5% Equity Increase (for two years)	$ 24,000
Total Increase in Value	$ 64,000
Total value of house	$264,000

Sources of Fix-up Houses

One of the great advantages of being a part-time investor is that there are good deals to be had even though you don't devote full attention to the job. The pros – the full-time investors - will get eye-popping deals, but there are still enough good left-over deals for us small time operators to get a share of the pie also. It's like a yard sale. The people who get the huge bargains will be up before dawn, knocking on doors before the yard sales are scheduled to start. Nevertheless, there are still some bargains left when the rest of us show up a little later in the morning. Finding good fix-up deals primarily involves reading the newspaper, checking the Internet, and driving through neighborhoods.

A good source of fix-up houses are those repossessed by banks. These are houses where the owner cannot make the payments on his bank loan and is forced to leave the house when the bank takes it from them. Often the former owner will express his bad feelings toward the bank by destroying fixtures, doors, walls and other parts of the house. While this may give the house an unlivable appearance, most of the damage is fairly easy to repair. This is just the type of house the aspiring investor is looking for, as it has built-in equity because the damage is only superficial.

A second source of good fix-up properties is from the Veteran's Administration (VA) and Housing and Urban Development (HUD). These properties have had owners who cannot make payments on their loans from these respective organizations, and the VA and HUD have repossessed the houses and put them back on the market. VA and HUD houses are usually offered at a fairly good price, below market if they need serious fix up work done. As in bank repos, the owners have either let their houses run down and are generally in need of, at minimum a paint job, and sometimes a more major fix-up. I purchased a VA home in a nice neighborhood that scared off many other investors because there had been water damage to the ceiling in both bathrooms. Upon close examination, I traced the damage to some cracks in the water cooler on the roof. Was it worth it to pay $100,000 for a house in a neighborhood where similar houses sold for $140,000? You bet it was. I could replace the cooler and repair the ceiling for $2,000 to $3,000. The remaining $37,000 of equity went to the only person who took the time to climb up on the roof and thoroughly examine the cooler with a flashlight. That was me. HUD, VA and repossessed houses from other federal agencies can be found at the following HUD website:

http://www.hud.gov/homes/homesforsale.cfm

To find bank repos and other fix-up houses my wife

and I carefully scan the newspaper classified ads every day and we spend weekends driving around areas where we might like to buy. We bought our first bank repo by responding to an ad in the newspaper. Based on the ad, it appeared to match all of our requirements, a fix-up house priced at below-market in a nice neighborhood. I visited the property, made an offer and purchased the property. I had my handyman friend go over with me to look over the property to give me a reliable second opinion.

To purchase VA and HUD repos, you can also pick up printed listing from real estate agents, some of whom specialize in such sales. Recently repossessed homes are generally listed every two weeks.

5

Paying For Your Fix-up Properties

Follow the freeway that leads to wealth by harnessing the secret force of capitalism – the power of borrowed money.

-William Nickerson

Getting Ahead on Borrowed Money

If you are an average person, making an average wage, you cannot expect to be involved in purchasing investment property without borrowing money. Without loans you would spend most of your adult life just saving enough money to purchase your private residence, and never have enough for investing.

There are two ways to get the money you need to buy your first fix-up property:

1.) Take out a new loan, using savings for a down payment,

2.) Refinance your existing home and use the proceeds to buy, or make a down payment on, a fix-up property.

Technique 1: Take Out A New Loan

This is how I paid for my first fix-up property. I had previously contacted the three major credit reporting companies and determined that my credit rating was good. Since it was my first investment house, I followed the advice of the real estate agent that was selling the property and took out a loan through a mortgage company that the agent already worked with. At that time, I had not developed the two-bid approach that was discussed in Chapter 3, which would have saved me some money. As a result, I paid more in interest than I should have. Two years later, I refinanced the original loan to lower my interest rate and to get some more investment money.

Let Leverage Work for You

One of the big advantages of real estate is that it allows you to make a lot of money by investing a little money. In almost any other investment field, be it stocks or starting a business, you have to invest 100% of the money required to do business. In real estate, because of the ability to use leverage, or to control loan money with only a relatively small down payment, you are able to get more investment "bang for the buck."

Let's look at an example. If you wanted to buy a $160,000 house and you were in the unlikely position of being able to pay the full price, you would not be using leverage. If the value of your property went up by 5% a year (the 60-year average), you would have a house worth $168,000 in one year. You would have an increase in equity, or a potential profit, of $8,000 (not counting closing costs, fix-up costs or tax breaks for now). You could take that profit out by refinancing or by selling the house, as we'll examine later. Table 5.1 illustrates this transaction.

Table 5.1 **No Leverage Purchase**	
Purchase price	$160,000
Down payment	0
Total cost	160,000
Value after 1 year	168,000
Increased equity	8,000
Profit on investment	5%

Now let's look at an example where leverage is used. This time the investor buys the same house for the same

$160,000 but he puts only $8,000 down, or 5%, and the mortgage company pays the rest in the form of a loan. (At one point, loans could be had for as low as 0% down, but down payment amounts change with the state of the economy.) After one year, the investor would again show an $8,000 profit for his investment, despite only investing 5% of the money he did in the previous example. Again, all other costs and tax breaks set aside for the sake of simplicity, the investor has turned a 100% profit on his investment (Table 5.2).

Table 5.2 Purchase with Leverage	
Purchase price	$160,000
Down payment	8,000
Total cost	160,000
Value after 1 year	168,000
Increased equity	8,000
Profit on investment	100%

Let's look at another scenario where an investor purchases one fix-up house every other year for 10 years. The investor purchases the first house for $100,000. By the time he purchases the second house, and the value of the first has increased through repairs and appreciation (30% through repairs and 5% per year through appreciation), the value of the first house has gone up to $143,500. If the value continues to go up 5% each year, by the end of 10 years the same house has increased in value to $210,100 (Table 5.3). The other houses increase at the same 5% yearly rate until the total equity of all houses at the end of the ten years is $376,100.

Table 5.3
Appreciation of Fix-up Houses Over Time

	House 1 value	House 2 value	House 3 value	House 4 value	House 5 value
Purchase price	$100,000				
After 2 years	$143,500	100,000			
After 4 years	$157,800	143,500	100,000		
After 6 years	$173,600	157,800	143,500	100,000	
After 8 years	$191,000	173,600	157,800	143,500	100,000
After 10 years	$210,100	191,000	173,600	157,800	143,500
EQUITY	$110,100	91,100	73,600	57,800	43,500

TOTAL EQUITY: $376,100

Technique 2: Refinance the Home that You Live In

Some people may find this option a little scary the first time they do it. I know that I did. I was worried that I might lose my home. But once I got my calculator out and saw how the deal would work out, I realized that I would be much better off by refinancing. And I still own the house that I first refinanced. I have long since moved to another house, but the original house is now one of my best rental properties. In doing your calculations, you must make sure that your new loan does not increase your monthly payments beyond what you can afford to pay. This is especially an issue when interest rates are rising. When interest rates are dropping, you may be able to refinance an existing loan and *lower* your monthly payments. The advantage of refinancing is that you can get enough money to make a down payment on a new loan and have enough leftover to pay for fix-up costs.

Your Credit Rating Could Make or Break You

If you have a good credit rating, it's fairly easy to get a loan from a bank or a mortgage company. If you haven't already done so, get copies of your credit report and carefully review them. If you have bad credit, you will need to get it fixed. If you have good credit, protect your rating like its gold because for a real estate investor, that's what it is. Your ability to get loans at a good interest rate and with low fees (or even to get a loan at all) depends on your credit rating. Eventually you will have enough cash to finance your house purchases, but initially you must depend upon loans to purchase houses.

A recent study in California found that 70% of home purchasers do not know what their credit rating is. Credit suppliers are required to disclose credit information to borrowers, including credit scores. But you shouldn't wait for the loan company to supply the information to you about your credit score. You need to know your score long before you ever apply for a loan. Anyone who has taken out loans and has a payment history will have a credit report on file with the three main credit-reporting bureaus: Equifax, Experian and TransUnion.

Your credit report is a report of all credit accounts, your payment status, and your current balance on each account and other information. The important thing is your credit score. The most common credit score is called the FICO score. FICO calculates a score ranging from 300 to 850, with about 60 percent of people having a score above 700. People with scores less than 620 are a considered a higher risk and will be charged higher fees and a higher interest rate. You should order credit reports from all three credit bureaus. The addresses are:

www.equifax.com
www.experian.com
www.transunion.com

Author Kathy Kristof, identifies the following factors that determine you credit score:

1.) How well you have paid your bills in the past,

2.) How much debt you have in relation to your available credit,

3.) How much experience you have in managing credit,

4.) How you managed different kinds of credit,

5.) Have you applied for many new credit lines in a short period of time; which may indicate someone who is likely to file for bankruptcy.

How to Improve Your Credit Score

After first ordering copies of your credit reports, you can then take steps to improve your score, if necessary. Some ways to improve your credit score include:

1. Pay all loan payments and credit card payments on time. If you are late, don't miss any more payments. The longer you pay on time the better your score.

2. Contact your loan companies or credit card companies if you have late payments on your report. Ask them how to have

this late payment information removed from your credit report.

3. Keep low credit card balances and keep as few credit card accounts open as possible. In many cases the more money you owe, or can potentially borrow through credit cards, the lower your score.

Private Mortgage Insurance

Investors who cannot afford a 20% down payment ($20,000 on a $100,000 loan) generally have to pay private mortgage insurance (PMI). Very few people want to tie up that much money in a down payment. PMI is a way for the lender to protect himself in case the buyer cannot make his monthly payments, and defaults on the loan.

Getting rid of PMI isn't always easy or automatic. It's in the interest of the lender to keep receiving the payments, even in some cases long after the purchaser has paid off the 20 percent required to remove PMI. It's up to the purchaser to take the initiative to have it removed by contacting the lender and asking how to have it removed. Getting PMI removed requires having an appraisal done on you house, to show that the value has appreciated, or by paying off 20% of the purchase price of the property.

Rate Sheets and Risk

Such factors as collateral, credit history, ability to repay the loan, and amount of cash on hand all determine how much you pay for your loan. One critical component in getting a loan that is less clearly understood by most applicants is the area of "rate sheets".

Rate sheets are what lenders use to set the interest rate that borrowers receive for their loans. The more risk factors that a borrower has, the more points they have to pay, and ultimately the higher the interest rate. One point is one percent of the loan amount.

Table 5.4 (adapted from *Real Estate Debt Can Make You Rich* by Steve Dexter) shows an example of some of the risk factors that are considered by loan officers, and the points that each risk factor could cost you.

Table 5.4 Rate Sheet Example	
Risk Factor	Points
credit score below 620	0.5 points
non-owner occupied with 75-80% down	2.0 points
loan amount <$100,000	0.5 points
loan amount <%50,000	1.5 points
manufactured home	0.5 points

In this example, for a $200,000 loan, if you had a credit score of 600 (costing 0.5 points) and you were purchasing a manufactured home (also costing 0.5 points); you would pay one additional point for your loan, or $2,000 (1% of the loan amount).

6

The Zen of Repairing Properties

There is no need to run outside
For better seeing,
Nor to peer from a window. Rather abide
At the center of your being;
For the more you leave it, the less you learn.

-Lao Tzu

Inner Growth and Making Repairs

Beyond the economic side of the fix-up business, there is a spiritual side to repairing houses. It's not just about making money or repairing houses. It's also about growing as a person.

In the above quote from the book "The Way of Life" author Lao Tzu points the way to a fulfilling life. The phrase "abide at the center of your being," to me means to focus on doing the things in life that are most important to our core self, who we really are underneath it all. At a basic level we all desire to learn, grow and create. Applied to our work with fix-up properties, we desire to humbly fix things and by small gradations create a better world both inside and outside of ourselves. When we abide at the center of our being we recognize that we are on the right path through the feeling of satisfaction that we have.

There is a deep satisfaction that I receive whenever I am able to repair something at a property I have purchased. I often get an inner glow that lasts for hours, sometimes days. This is especially true when I have made a repair that I have never done before. After I finish the project, I bask in the warmth of satisfaction and the overwhelming feeling of confidence that "anything is possible".

Before I began doing fix-up properties, many times my attempts at even minor repairs ended up in failure. I thought that it was just beyond my abilities to understand the complexities of this type of repair work. (I admit that I didn't do that much physical labor around the house. In fact, about the only exercise I got was in jumping to conclusions, dangling participles and splitting infinitives.) I often felt that in any confrontation between myself and the mysterious electrical system, the byzantine plumbing system or perplexing carpentry work, that I would always be the loser.

There is also an inherent fear of failure that often saps our energy and forces us to not even attempt what we may fear is a difficult repair. By charging ahead in spite of our fears we often realize that, after removing a cover or digging into a project, the solution is self-evident. I've often found that the problem is solved fairly easily by attaching a loose wire or unclogging a pipe. The worst case scenario is that I just have to replace something that is broken, which isn't so difficult when you have a book to refer to or can discuss it with an "expert" at a hardware store.

On the first property that I purchased, I hired out almost all of the technical repairs and focused my efforts on landscaping and painting. On the second property that I purchased I began diving into the technical repairs more. I wired the front porch light myself after having hired someone else to do it on the first property. The installation went slowly, since I was just learning, but the satisfaction I received was a big boost to my confidence. Beyond the satisfaction, I was surprised at how easy it was. Before starting, I had images of causing irreparable damage to the house. From that inauspicious start, I went on to other wiring projects. I put ceiling fans in all the rooms. Then I put a hall light in and installed a doorbell. I put electrical receptacles in the bathroom and installed new switches. Each accomplishment gave me more confidence and wet my appetite for more. Now, I don't think twice about doing almost any electrical repair that comes up.

The great inner truths of repairing houses are, like learning all great truth and wisdom, only revealed gradually. Some of the skills that must be learned and exercised in the course of fixing up a house include:

- Patience
- Strength
- Persistence
- Creativity
- Self-knowledge
- Overcoming fears
- Openness to learning

One of the greatest feelings of satisfaction is looking at your house after you have spent countless hours fixing it up. I sometimes think, "Wow, it's hard to believe that I have returned the house to its original condition." It's almost magical. Before getting started in fix-up houses, I could never have imagined being able to do something like that. Over the years of having to put the same houses back together again after tenants have beat them up, you find it gets easier and faster to repair them each time. You feel like a doctor who brings a patient back to health.

Work Like Dogs, Eat Like Hogs, Sleep Like Logs

As Lincoln said, some people will try to convince you that "A horse chestnut is the same as a chestnut horse." And some self-proclaimed "experts" will try to convince you that operating a real estate business is a piece of cake. Don't believe them. If it was easy, everybody would be doing it.

Fixing up is hard work. Don't expect it to be easy. Many a day my wife and I work for long hours after our regular jobs. Then, we work early the next morning before the kids are up, until it is time to go to our day jobs. My brother, my wife and I spent full weekends painting until our arms were so tired that we couldn't hold a brush. We worked like dogs, we ate like hogs, and we slept like logs.

I don't need to tell you that life is not always fair. We don't always get rewarded for the things we do, like working overtime and weekends at our 9:00-5:00 job. But in the case of the fix-up business, hard work and dedication are rewarded through the new skills that we learn and when the rental checks come in.

Learning the Skills

Just as when you are leaning other aspects about buying a house, you should be gathering information about house repairs everywhere you go. Never let an opportunity pass to learn. Buy books and videos on house repair. I like to scour the fix-up book areas at used book stores for good buys. I buy a book as soon as I see it if I know that it has valuable information. In the past, I have waited to purchase the book only to return later and find that the book I had wanted was gone. The price you pay will literally be a drop in the bucket compared to the money you will save. (For a list of books and videos that I use, see Appendix C)

Go to free classes on household projects at home improvement stores like *Home Depot* and *Lowe's*. Sometimes you'll get personalized attention. Once I attended a class on installation of ceiling fans at *Home Depot* and I was the only person to show up. I was able to learn everything I needed to know and I installed the demonstration model during the class while the instructors talked me through it. In another class I watched a demonstration on how to install floor tiles in a bathroom floor and then went to my house and did it myself. I also learned to make other repairs by reading books and watching videos.

My brother, Mike, and I installed our first tiling project in a small bathroom. It couldn't be described as "perfect," but it was a pretty good start. And, I got better each time I do it. My wife and I have since tiled larger rooms, learning to be more efficient each time, and savings hundreds of dollars on each job.

Community colleges usually offer courses in the building trades, with both classroom and hands-on experience. You can take courses at night, while still working your day job. I have learned much from classes in electrical wiring, plumbing and carpentry.

Since you are constantly visiting open houses, take note of repairs and improvements done in their houses. Don't be afraid to copy what others have done or adapt it to your house. Imitation is the sincerest form of flattery.

Draw on the Past

After I got more involved in the repair work of our houses, I thought back about how my father had taught me a lot by example. I recall seeing him construct screened-in porches on various houses that we had lived in. I was too young to help out much at the time, or to appreciate what he was doing, but looking back I realize that it required a strong desire to learn the basic principals, and a sense of self-confidence to build it. He had no formal training in construction, and didn't have reference books like I do, but he learned by observing other porches that had been built in the neighborhood.

My mother is also quite adept at making household repairs, and quite willing to get involved in the process as well. Her specialty is making repairs with only the materials she has at hand. I've lost count of how many things are held together at her house with essentially just thin wire and thumb tacks. You too may have family members that you can draw inspiration from when it comes to making repairs.

What to Fix Up

A key to fixing up a house is to know when to stop fixing up. You want the house to look good, yet you know that people are not going to care for your house the same way that you would. For rental properties, I replace things at the lowest cost possible, yet ensuring that it still looks good. If I know that I am going to sell the house I will install higher grade of materials, especially where it really counts, like the kitchens and bathrooms. As Lawrence Dworin says in *Profits in Buying & Renovating Homes*:

> It's easy to get carried away on renovation projects – wasting time and money on repairs that buyers won't pay extra for. I assume you like to do good work. We all do. And we'd like every finished project to be a showplace. But you can't make money that way. Your buyers have a limit on what they're willing to pay. That's why you've got to limit repair costs. I call that cost control. In this business, cost control means concentrating on fixing code violations and creating a clean, safe, livable house.

Just as in learning other skills in this business, it takes time to develop your skills. I didn't begin my business with a background in construction, so like everything else I picked it up as I went along. For the first property that my wife and I bought we relied on a great handyman to do much of the work. Some of the additional work was also contracted out such as some electrical wiring and repair of broken windows. What my wife and I focused on in the first house was caulking holes and cracks in the walls, painting inside and out, and landscaping. Fortunately, our handyman was willing to coach us so that we picked up a many new skills along the way.

What should you focus on repairing in a fix-up house? Of course it depends upon what kind of shape the house is in. In general, for many fix-up houses, caulking holes and giving the whole house a good coat of paint goes a long ways to make it look good. As mentioned, key parts of the house to focus on when deciding what to repair are bathrooms and kitchens. Bathrooms and kitchens are what we men often overlook. But if you want to appeal to the women, you'd better have the bathrooms and kitchens in great shape.

Kitchens need to look bright and should be painted with a light color of paint, like white. In fact, my preference is to use white, or an off-white like Swiss Coffee, throughout the house. But if the kitchen is a dark color, I would repaint it in white. If they are not completely worn out, you can usually just paint the cabinets and change the handles and hinges. If the cabinets are too far gone, check the second-hand building materials stores (see more on these stores in Chapter 10) for inexpensive used cabinets and put them in. I usually put used refrigerators into my rentals. Vinyl tiles are a good choice to use in rental properties for dining rooms and kitchens. Individual vinyl tiles are easier to replace than is one large piece of vinyl.

Bathrooms also need a newer appearance. Tubs should always be sparkling clean. I usually put in a new medicine cabinet and re-caulk the tub since the old caulk is black and brittle. If it's a cement floor, think about putting in tiles. Toilets and sinks are fairly easy to replace. I have gotten good toilets at second-hand building materials stores also.

Naturally, anything that is broken must be repaired or replaced, preferably the former. I like to replace the electrical outlets and switches in the house if they are old or outdated. I usually put ceiling fans in all of the rooms and replace old-fashioned ceiling lights and hall lights with newer, yet inexpensive, ones. These are all relatively inexpensive improvements that can greatly improve the overall appearance of a house.

I prefer to cover rather than replace old flooring. For example, you can buy left-over pieces of carpet from a carpet store cheaply, to cover old-fashioned tile on a bedroom floor. And, you can buy inexpensive laminate flooring to cover old tile, or bad-looking cement, floors. Watch for sales of laminate flooring at home improvement stores and buy it when it is cheap.

Safety First

When repairing homes always remember to put your safety first. If you haven't done so, I recommend taking an OSHA (Occupational Safety and Health Administration) class. I took that class in connection with my building trades classes at the junior college. You can take a 10 hour course and get it over with in one day. If you don't have the background in the building trades, as I didn't, it will make you aware of many unforeseeably dangers and show you how to establish a safe working environment.

It is also important to comply with building codes. Ignorance of the law is no excuse. If you install plumbing, electrical wiring, or walls that are not up to code, you may wind up tearing them out again and having it done correctly. Refer to code books found in public libraries, or buy your own copy. If work is not done to code, not only is it a violation of the law, but it can also be dangerous to the people living in your house.

Avoid Perfectionism

Where safety is an issue where you don't want to cut corners, for other areas you should look for ways to cut corners and save money. Don't let "perfect" be the enemy of "good" when making repairs. You don't need to repair everything that is wrong with a house. Don't be a perfectionist. Dworin points out:

> *Buyers don't scrutinize each item in a house.*
> *The look at the whole package. They evaluate*
> *the overall condition of the house and compare*
> *it others they can afford. They won't notice little*
> *flaws in the cabinets, floor tile, paint job or*
> *woodwork. You're probably the only one who*
> *will notice defects like these.*

If it comes to a choice between spending excessive money to make the house perfect, and on the other hand taking the profits and running, then I for one, could do with the exercise (to paraphrase Douglas Adams in *The Hitchhikers Guide to the Galaxy*).

Tools of the Trade - "Give Me a Lever ... and I Shall Move the World"

In 400 B.C. Archimedes said, "Give me a lever long enough, and a fulcrum upon which to place it, and I shall move the world." Your tools and books are your lever and fulcrum. Once you have them there will be no stopping you.

You need a set of tools to do all the fix-up required for a house. I advocate gradually building up your tool arsenal. Buy the tools as the need arises. That way you spread the cost out and you don't have tools sitting around that you never use. Some tools that you will need at minimum (beyond the basic hammer, saw, nails, etc.) are listed in Table 6.1. The list below could be pretty long, but I list just a few to give you an idea.

Table 6.1
Recommended Tools to Have on Hand

- Battery operated drill. The uses you will find for a good drill are limitless; drilling holes, and driving screws. Make sure you get a least one extra rechargeable battery so that work doesn't grind to a halt when the first battery goes dead. It is also good to have a cord powered drill as a backup.
- Cord powered drill to stir mortar and cement.
- Storage case of screws and bolts & nuts of various sizes. You can often buy the case, screws and all, at a hardware store. It will save you from making excessive trips to the hardware store.
- Miter box for cutting the corners on trim work.
- Electric saw to cut wood.
- Tile saw.
- Electric current tester for outlets.
- Pipe wrench for uncooperative pipes.
- Electrical multitester, for testing volts, amps and continuity.
- Level, to assure that boards are straight up and down.
- Adjustable square for marking straight lines.

For both rental fix-ups, as well as fix-up of new properties, I like to group my tools into tool boxes. This way, when I have to go to a rental property to make a repair, I just grab the appropriate tool box without having to scrounge around for tools. The tool boxes I have pre-loaded include:

Electrical tool box - contains wire stripper, voltage detector, pliers, screw drivers, electrical tape, multi-tester, stud finder, continuity tester, needle nose pliers, linesman's pliers and wire nuts.

Plumbing tool box - contains pipe wrenches, sink washers, adjustable wrench, box wrenches, PVC cutting tool, and PVC glue.

Roofing tool box - joint trowel, screw driver, steel-toothed hand-broom, plenty of cloth and towels. In a plastic grocery bag I also carry plastic mesh and tools with roofing cement on them. I also carry cans of roofing cement separately.

I also carry the basic tools such as the drill, screwdriver, nuts & bolts box, to any job.

As you get more proficient and take on bigger repair tasks, eventually you will need more powerful tools, like the table saw. I bought a table saw to make the cuts on laminate flooring. A word of warning, table saws can be very dangerous to use, as can other tools, when not operated properly. Be sure to follow all safety precautions. Table saws are particularly dangerous because the motor is so powerful that it can pull your hand into the blade. The saw can also kick pieces of wood at you at high speeds. Even people with years of experience using the table saw have suffered serious injuries. If it can happen to them, it can happen to you. Take your time and observe all safety precautions. Always put safety first.

In the next chapter we turn our attention to two proven ways to make money in real estate.

7

The Two Safest Ways to Make Money in Real Estate

The people who get on in the world are the people who get up and look for the circumstances they want, and if they can't find them, make them.

-George Bernard Shaw

The two techniques that are the safest ways to make money in real estate are:

1.) turn your residence into a rental instead of selling it,

2.) sell a house that you live in for 2 years, and pay no income tax on the sale.

Technique 1: Turn Your Residence into a Rental Instead of Selling It

As mentioned earlier, one way to obtain investment money to purchase fix-up houses is by refinancing a house that you already own. Refinancing a house means to take out a new loan on your rental property, or home, that replaces the existing loan.

When purchasing a fix-up investment property, you may decide not to sell your principal residence, but instead turn it into a rental property. This approach makes it easier to do repairs to the rental house because, having lived there, you know the short cuts and tricks of how to fix the things that typically need repair.

A system that I like to use is to refinance my residence about a year before I plan to buy a new residence. This gives me enough money for a down payment on the next house that I will purchase. When I locate a good fixer-upper I can quickly purchase it. During the 3-4 weeks it takes to close on the new house, I prepare the old house so it will be ready to rent. This usually involves some painting and landscaping. Then, before I close on the new house, the "for rent" sign goes up on the old house.

The three steps in this technique are:

1.) refinance your residence.
2.) use the refinance money as a down payment to buy a new house.
3.) move into the new house and rent out the old house

Instead of refinancing your residence, you can use money from savings or a loan from a relative or a friend, as a down payment. As mentioned, an advantage of refinancing your residence while you are still living there is that you get a lower interest rate on your loan than if you were refinancing a rental property.

When I did my first refinancing of a townhouse that I owned, I received a rate of 6.1%. The rate for my original loan was 7.5%. The original purchase price was $52,500 but the value had increased to $82,000 ten years later (Table 7.2). I had also paid off about $10,000 of the mortgage principal over the course of the ten years.

Table 7.2 Townhouse Refinancing	
Original purchase price	$52,500
Principal pay down	$10,000
Value ten years later	$82,000
Amount of equity in house	$39,500 (82,000 - 52,500 - 10,000)
Less 20% of value (to avoid PMI)	$16,400
Total amount of cash back	$23,100 (39,500 - 16,400)

When refinancing, you should keep 20 percent of the value of the house in the house to avoid paying private mortgage insurance and to pay a lower interest rate. After refinancing the townhouse, my monthly mortgage payments went down from $535 per month to $518 per month. Normally, you pay 1 percent extra if you refinance as an investor instead of as an owner occupant. Although with good credit and by shopping around, it's possible to have the 1 percent waived.

Timing Your Refinancing

Refinancing your mortgage loans is another aspect of real estate that will require you to develop some expertise and close attention to the details of the economy and interest rates. I have heard investors recommend refinancing every chance you get, regardless of interest rates, and to take out as much money as you can. That philosophy is dangerous because you want to avoid raising your monthly payments beyond the point where you can afford to pay them.

While refinancing is a common way for real estate investors to tap into the equity in their houses, you must be careful not to take out a large loan that increases your monthly payments beyond what you take in on rent. If you see that rents are going up in your area and you can increase rents enough to cover the monthly payments on a refinancing, then go ahead and refinance to take some of money out of a house. Ideally, that money is used to purchase more investment property. However, if your rents will not cover the refinancing payments, don't put yourself in the awkward (and perilous) position of having to lose money every month.

Monitoring interest rates will also help you decide when to refinance. When interest rates are dropping, like they were in the early 2000's, you were able to refinance a house, take money out, and lower your monthly payments. That was a real estate investor's dream. As interest rates started rising again later on, it required investors to be more cautious in refinancing.

Technique 2: Sell a House that You Live in for Two Years and Pay No Income Tax

The 1997 Taxpayer Relief Act was a great boost for average people who wanted to sell their home and buy a new one. It was also a great boost for investors. Couples are allowed to exclude up to $500,000 of the capital gain on the sale of their primary residence. Single individuals can exclude up to $250,000. In other words, the sale of the house is never reported on your federal IRS forms if the capital gain is less than the $500,000 and $250,000 limits. This exclusion is based on compliance with two requirements:

1. The home must have been the primary residence for both spouses during two of the last five years. The two years do not have to be consecutive but if you rent out the primary residence for more than three years you would be required to occupy it again for two years.

2. The exclusion is available only once every two years.

Capital gains above $250,000 for singles and $500,000 for couples are taxed at the applicable rate. For a complete description of how to use the exemption, see Internal Revenue Service Publication 523 *Selling Your Home.*

What if you sell your house before meeting the two year requirement? If you qualify under one of the unforeseen events listed in the IRS publication, such as a job change, illness or an unusual hardship, you can still qualify for a prorated exclusion. Check Publication 523 for a complete list of unforeseen circumstances, at:

http://www.irs.gov/pub/irs-pdf/p523.pdf

What This Mean for Investors

Utilization of this tax exemption is the safest investment strategy for the conservative investor who wants to take few risks. This is the type of investor who wears both suspenders and a belt to hold up his pants. They like to play it safe. Under this strategy, the investors can qualify for the least expensive loan, the owner-occupied loan. There is no need to worry about tenants destroying your rental property or not paying the rent. You completely control the investment by living in the property yourself. When you sell, you have the opportunity to bring in up to $500,000 tax-free money every two years.

Here is an example to show how the exclusion works, illustrated in Table 7.3. You and your wife file jointly and you continuously buy and sell homes over the years, each time purchasing a more expensive home as a replacement. Let's say that you bought a house for $300,000. For the last 5 years you have owned the home and it is now worth $600,000, with $300,000 worth of accumulated gain. If you were to sell your home now for $600,000, without the tax exemption you would be subject to a capital gains tax on $300,000. The amount of taxes saved with the tax exemption would be $84,000. Table 7.3 also illustrates other amounts of gains.

Table 7.3
Home Selling under the Taxpayer Relief Act
Exemption
(assuming a 28% tax bracket)

Home	purchase price	sales price	capital gain	tax saved
#1	$150,000	$200,000	$50,000	$14,000
#2	$200,000	$300,000	$100,000	$28,000
#3	$300,000	$600,000	$300,000	$84,000

Increase Cash Flow, Sell One House to Pay off Another

Cash flow is a key consideration in staying afloat financially for the real estate investor. One way to increase cash flow is to sell a house, utilizing the exclusion, and use the money from that house to pay the mortgage off on another property that you own. It works best when you pay off a house that only has a relatively small mortgage left. For example, if you sell your principal residence for $250,000, you might receive $150,000, after paying off the existing mortgage of $100,000. With that money, you could pay off the mortgage on another property that you own, with say $50,000, and use the remaining $100,000 as a down payment on one or two other fix-up properties. If you had been paying $700 per month for the mortgage on the other property, and receiving $800 in rent, you would now be able to receive the entire $800 in rent without having to pay the mortgage. This way you have increased your cash flow by $700 per month (not counting taxes and insurance).

Know When to Sell

If you do sell your primary residence, you should try to time it to maximize your profits. There are cycles in the economy and you can increase the amount you sell your house for if you are aware of the cycles. As John W. Schaub in *Building Wealth One House at a Time* wisely points out, "Buy when it's hard to sell and sell when everyone wants to buy." When housing prices are dropping and many people are trying to sell house, it is a buyers market and buyers have the upper hand in negotiating a price. When housing prices are rising and more people want to buy houses, fewer houses are available. It is a sellers market and sellers have the advantage in price negotiations. When possible, sell during a sellers market.

Combining Techniques to Create Synergy

Combine technique 1 and technique 2 to get even more powerful results. Here is what to do. 1) Refinance your primary residence to get down payment money for a new property. 2) Buy a fix-up property and move into it. 3) Live in the new property 2 to 5 years while fixing it up. Then sell it, taking advantage of the Taxpayer Relief Act exemption and pay no federal income tax. 4) Use the income from that sale as a down payment to buy a more expensive fix-up house.

8

Renting Out Houses: Bait the Hook and Reel in the Fish

Never be afraid to try something new
Remember, amateurs built the Ark; professionals built the
Titanic

Curb Appeal

From the perspective of the potential tenant, you must have what the real estate agents call "curb appeal", or a house that is attractive from the street. Anyone passing by should not just take a passing glance at the house; your house must look so good that they say to themselves, "I would like to live there!" This involves planning and work on your part, but pays off with a house that rents more quickly.

To get your house in condition for renting requires a fresh coat of paint outside, and possibly inside. My wife and I like to put colorful flowers in the flower garden and pots of beautiful flowers along the sidewalk that leads to the front door. Flowers add color and a sense of freshness to a house.

Make any repairs that you are aware of before the tenants move into the house. This includes, leaky faucets, toilets that don't flush right, roof leaks and termites. If you don't do it now, you're bound to get a call from your tenants when you least want it (just when you're walking out the door for a family vacation). Put awnings in if you have a window facing a hot westerly direction, as is the case in Tucson. They are cheap, easy to install and will make the house much cooler and attractive.

Background Checks: Scrape Off Bad Applicants Like Barnacles

You must have a system to access the background and history of the person who wants to rent your house. Have all persons who are interested in renting your property fill out an application form, then after a week or two collecting applications select the tenants you like the best. This selection should be based on their ability to pay and your perception on how well they will take care of the house and be a good tenant. Always call their references and supervisors and past landlords to make sure they check out.

Find out all you can about the tenants while they look around the house. This helps in the screening and selection process. I like to casually ask where they work, do they have kids or dogs, and where are they coming from. Don't make it look like you are trying to give them the third degree. Share things about yourself as well.

Some of the things that I look for in a tenant include:

- they have a bank account.
- they have a steady job and make enough money to pay the rent.
- don't have pit bulls, or other dangerous dogs. You don't want to be held liable for the actions of your tenant's dogs.
- they communicate with you. I had an applicant who barely spoke to me when he and his wife looked at the house. Then when he filled out the application form, he didn't fill in all of the blanks. That sent up red flags to me that he was trying to hide something, maybe a criminal record or bad credit. If you don't have a good feel for an applicant it's best to avoid later tenant problems and find someone else to rent the house.
- they don't have more than one car per tenant. Nothing makes a house look junky faster than a lot of cars parked around it.
- they seem inclined to take care of the outdoor plants.

In addition to references, be sure to investigate applicant's run-ins with the law at the county Consolidated Justice Courts web page, which many cities have, found in Tucson at:

http://geronimo.jp.co.pima.az.us/casesearch/

Type in their last name and select the type of court case you would like to search. The options include: traffic cases, civil cases (where one person takes another person to court to collect money for damages) and criminal cases.

When renting out a house recently, I received two almost equally qualified applicants. One of the two was very eager to rent the house and was ready to put down a deposit as soon as she saw it. I told her my policy was to collect applications through Friday and then decide next week after calling the references of the best applicants. The first thing I did the following week was to check the justice court web page to see if they had ever broken the law. It turned out that the eager applicant had four traffic violations on record and two civil cases against her involving housing. Since the rest of the information that I had about the two applicants was equally positive, the information from the courts helped me to select the best tenant.

You can also hire a prescreening agency to conduct a background check for a fee. You will need the applicant's social security number and their consent to run a check. One prescreening service is provided by mrlandlord.com. For $9.95, they will send you an instant credit report (For us smaller rental property owners we must also pay an annual fee of $59). They can also provide eviction report, security traces and criminal reports. These services can be found at:

www.MrLandlord.com

Rental Contracts

I have a system of rewards and penalties in my contract. If the tenants pay on time (by the 1st of the month), they receive a discount of $15 to $25. If the rent is $715, they pay only $700 for that month. On the other hand, if they pay late, they must pay 1% of the amount due for each day the rent is late ($7 a day), in addition to not receiving the discount. In your rental contract, it saves headaches down the road if you include a pre-pay discount clause such as this. This is all the motivation that many tenants need to pay on time.

I include clauses describing unauthorized activities that could result in their expulsion, such as:

- loud music or parties (you don't want the tenants to disturb the neighbors).
- additional persons or pets living at the house that are not listed on their application.
- not taking care of the yard.
- extensive car repairs on the property.

I also include clauses stating that if the full rent is not paid after the fifth day agreed upon, I have the right to remove the tenant from the house. I have a clause that I can enter the house at reasonable times for inspections. I like to include a clause prohibiting waterbeds, and requiring that I be notified when house repairs are needed. Most state law favors the tenants not the landlords. These additional clauses are designed to protect the landlord. The goal is that you keep a close eye on your property and manage it carefully.

Always state that the security deposit will be used to cover unpaid rent, damages, repair and cleaning of the premises. I state that $150 of the $700 deposit is non-refundable and is used to sanitize, clean and repair the house. If the $150 non-refundable deposit doesn't cover all cleaning and repair costs, then it comes out of the remaining $550. I provide a year's supply of air conditioning and furnace filters for all of my rental properties. Unless filters are changed it can reduce the life of these expensive appliances. Despite the fact that I supply the filters, most of the time, the tenants still won't change them. So, periodically, whenever I go to house for a repair, to talk to the tenant for whatever reason, I also change the filter while I am there. That is the only way that I am sure that it gets done.

I have learned from experience that month-to-month leases are the best way to protect yourself against problem tenants. I used to have tenants sign a one-year, or even two-year, lease. I thought that it was a safe way to lock them into the lease. That works fine if you don't have any problems with your tenant. However, if you get a tenant who doesn't pay, or pays late, you have to document that they have not paid if you want to go to court to get them removed. This means making copies of paychecks, notices and all correspondence with the tenant. You may invest many hours collecting documentation and you may still lose the case, or the tenant may move away before paying back rent.

It is much easier to get rid of a bad tenant with a month-to-month lease. All you need to do is to give them notice one month before you terminate the contract. Of course, the tenant can also terminate the contract by giving you a one month notice. That's alright with me because if the tenant is not happy they won't take care of the place. I'd rather have a happy tenant in there that can pay the rent.

In dealing with the legalities of deal with tenants, a good reference book is the *Arizona Landlord's Deskbook*. Other states have similar books. This book provides a wealth of information on how to legally deal with tenants in various common situations. You learn to anticipate and deal with problems before they occur. This is done primarily by clearly stating the exact behavior that you expect (and demand) from your tenant in the rental contract. Problems occur when those types of behavior are not clearly spelled out. The book also provides easy to copy forms that you will need to deal with tenants.

Advertising

My wife and I used to advertise our rental houses in the city newspaper. We would also advertise in the university newspaper for a house we own near the university campus. A big source of our inquiries comes from a free apartment locator service. The service charges people a fee to help them find a rental property, but doesn't charge landlords anything to advertise. The locator service originally saw one of our ads in the newspaper and contacted us to ask if they could advertise it with their service as well. It is a useful service to help you to rent your house more quickly.

If you run a newspaper ad, you should keep it as simple as possible and communicate all the vital information so as to pre-screen callers. I like to a place a positive feature at the front of the ad to grab people's attention. For example, one property is a townhouse that is fairly large, so I wrote "Roomy townhouse" at the beginning of the ad. Initially, we ran an ad like this:

Roomy Townhouse. 2 bed/2 bath, W/D, A/C, carport, refrigerator. $800/mo. 324-1029.

Use abbreviations in your ads whenever possible, to save money. For example, you can use W/D for washer/dryer and A/C for air conditioning.

While the above techniques worked pretty well, in recent years, we have had great success in just fixing the houses up and putting our "for rent" sign in the front yard of the properties, with an information sheet taped to the front window. On the information sheet I list the price, the number of rooms, appliances and other features, and I put my cell phone number on the sheet for people to call. An attractive house in a convenient, not necessarily expensive, location is the best advertisement that you can have.

Open Houses: Attract Tenants Like Flies

A rental "open house" is a good way to attract tenants. An open house is good because 1) it focuses all the visits so we do not spend so much time traveling over to the house every time someone wanted to come by, and 2) you catch more people who just happen to be driving by on Saturday and Sunday and stop by. A third reason occurred to me later, that single women, single moms, or anyone for that matter, might feel more comfortable coming to an open house where a lot of people are present, rather than to a one-on-one meeting in an unfamiliar location. It takes the pressure off when someone can look around the house anonymously rather than be the focus of attention as the only looker.

Closing the Deal

Having selected the tenants you want, you are now ready to sign the contract. I usually do the signing in the house that they are renting. It's convenient and I can walk them through the house and show them where the air filters are, how to operate appliances, and quirks that the house may have.

This is the first and best opportunity that you have to tell them how you expect them to behave in your house. You will never have this opportunity to "lay down the law" with them again. It may take a while, but I go over the entire contract with them. If you give the contract to them before the signing they probably won't read it. They will assume that all rental contracts are basically alike. They won't know that your contract has been modified by you to include clauses that protect your property. As I go over the property, I read everything to them, but I emphasize heavily certain parts. In particular, I emphasize and I repeat several times that I must receive the monthly rent payment by the first of the month. If the payment is not on time, they do not receive the discounted rate and they pay 1% of the rent for each day that the rent is late. I tell them that we evict them from the property if the rent is not paid by the fifth of the month.

In reality, it's not so bad if they pay late, but you don't want them to know that. For one late-paying tenant that I presently have, this means an additional $100 each month, or $1200 per year. He always pays late, but he knows that he must always pay the penalty too. I would only evict them if they paid late and didn't pay the penalty. In that case, where they don't pay the penalty charges, it's not worth it for me to let them stay in the house. If they don't think you are serious at the beginning, they will pay you late and not pay the penalty. Other things will take precedence over paying you, such as, buying new TVs, video game players, computers, making car payments and taking vacations. The tenants must know that penalties will be applied if they don't pay.

Irene and Mike Milin also take the contract signing process seriously. In their book, *How to Buy and Manage Rental Properties*, they state, "we make sure each applicant understands the agreement thoroughly and completely. This is why we spend as much as an hour and a half with each prospect, and go over the agreement line by line and word by word when necessary. We gauge their responses, and then we decide whether or not they passed the interview."

Another key part of the contract that I extensively go over with the tenants is the need to return the property clean to us. I tell them that we have spent great time and effort to make the house clean and in good operating condition for them and that we expect the house to be returned to us in the same condition. If not, we will use as much of their security deposit as we need to bring the house back up to that condition.

Some tenants think that it is a "sacred right" that they receive their security deposit back at the end of the lease. They believe that by mopping the floors and vacuuming the carpet they have completed their contract responsibilities. They don't think about the dirty ovens, broken tiles, chipped paint, moldy bathroom caulk, broken fence post and many other repairs that my wife and I have to do to get the house ready for the next tenant. By going into detail about what we expect at the end contract, I relieve tenants of the "sacred right" misconception.

At the signing, you collect the damage deposit and the check for the first month's rent. You should give them a check-off inspection list for them to fill out and return to you. This protects you if they damage the property. You can go back to the list to show that they didn't list any damage when they moved in.

I also like to give the tenants a list of things that are useful to know about the house, such as, when the trash is picked up, how often to change filters, emergency numbers to call, when the rental check is due, and my phone number and PO Box. If your house was built before 1977 you must provide the tenants with a lead-based paint pamphlet to warn them of the dangers of lead-based paint. You can download a copy at:

http://www.hud.gov/offices/lead/leadhelp.cfm.

Dealing with Problem Tenants

Filling the role of a landlord will be a true test of your resolve to be a real estate investor. The major reason that many people are deterred from purchasing real estate property is because of the prospect of having to deal with bad tenants. I can assure you that at some time your resolve will be tested. You will have to deal with tenants who don't pay on time, or who don't take care of your house. It is an unavoidable experience that happens to everyone, and one that you can learn a lot from.

There are two responses that I have when dealing with problem tenants. First, I tell myself that the "pain is worth the gain." In other words, just accept the difficulties and remember that no matter how much trouble this person is, they are still helping to build my wealth. They pay down my principal each month, which will eventually allow me to pay off the mortgage. A little unpleasantness is a small price to pay for the financial security that I receive.

My second response is to take the dealings with a problem tenant lightly (assuming of course that they are not destroying your house or doing something illegal). Joke about their excuses for not paying on time. Keep a list of excuses to share with other landlords. Problem tenants are usually the number one topic of conversation when landlords get together. If you take the perspective that it's just a natural part of the process and view it in a humorous vein, your blood pressure will be much lower and you will weather the storm without too much wear and tear.

In addition to having the right mental attitude mentioned above, you must also be diligent in dealing with tenants who don't pay on time. If their first rent is late, mail out a "pay or quit" form, advising them that they have 5 days to pay the rent, and the late fees, or they will be evicted. This form, and many other are available in the *Arizona Landlord's Deskbook*. In case they didn't get the message when you went over the contract with them, you must train your tenants from the start and show them that you are serious. If you don't strongly enforce the rules at the beginning, the first time it happens, the tenants will train you to take the rent checks whenever it is convenient for them, and not pay the penalty. Remember, they will have a million excuses to pay you late, while at the same time they spend their money on other things that are important to them but not to you. Make them face reality early and they will learn that they must pay on time, and if they don't, they pay penalties.

Noisy Tenants

If I receive complaints from neighbors that my tenants are being noisy, first I call them and tell them of the complaints, then I send the tenants the following letter.

Tenant name
Address
Notice of Material Noncompliance
Date

Dear *tenant name,*

This is a follow-up to my phone message to you yesterday. As I mentioned, I have received several complaints that you have been playing music too loudly in the house. This is a violation of the contract.

You are hereby notified pursuant to ARS §33-1368(A) that this constitutes a material noncompliance and that your right to possess and occupy the premises may be terminated, if this occurs again.

If you have any questions, contact my at 270-xxxx.

Terry Sprouse
Landlord

Dealing with problem tenants is something that you get better at with each new tenant. You learn to make corrections in the way you deal with tenants, to anticipate and avoid past unacceptable behavior. Don't get discouraged, it gets better with practice. I've said it before and I'll say it again here. Dealing with tenants requires fortitude. And, if you don't have fortitude, you have to use the next best thing – three-and-a-half-titude!

Five rules on how **not** to be successful in the repair and rent out business can be found in Table 8.1.

Table 8.1
The Five Rules on
How to Lose Money and Get Your Rental Property
Trashed by Your Tenants

Rule 1

Choose the worst possible area. The location of your investment property will determine the kinds of tenants you will attract, and how much rent you can fairly charge.

Rule 2

Put the very best of everything in when fixing up an investment property. Luxury bathrooms, thick pile carpets, plasma TVs. Never shop at stores that recycle construction supplies. Spare no expense.

Rule 3

Make sure you have absolutely no experience in making basic repairs. Not knowing how to change electrical outlets, unclog drains and toilets, and replace broken windows will cost you quite a bit of money down the road.

Rule 4

Do not screen your tenants. This may be the most important step to making sure you lose money as a landlord. Do not ask for or check references. Do not call previous landlords and ask questions like, did they pay rent on time? How was the condition of the house or apartment when they left? Did they ever disturb neighbors with loud music or shouting matches? How often would you have to make special trips for repairs? Being as uninformed as possible about whom you rent to will make a huge difference and will increase the chances that you will get tenants that will trash your property and refuse to pay rent.

Rule 5
Make sure you have not learned about your rights as a landlord. Be completely unfamiliar with the eviction process to guarantee long, drawn out disputes with tenants. Don't keep up to date financial records or copies of correspondence with your tenants. Most states provide online information about tenant and landlord rights so avoid reading these.

(Adapted from Andrew Stefanczyk posting on Investalist.co.uk)

Insurance and Invisibility: Layers of Protection for Your Properties and Yourself

In order to provide some protection to your investments and your family, it's a good idea to protect your assets by putting up obstacles for people who may wish to make you a target.

The first layer of protection should be an insurance policy that protects your assets if someone sues you. If someone trips on a rug in one of your rental properties, and decides to try and hold you liable, your insurance company should defend you in court. If they don't, you sue the insurance company. I have the standard $300,000 protection on each of my rental houses. Some people keep a $1 million umbrella policy. You will have to decide how much protection you need.

A second way to protect yourself and your family from a hostile client or from someone else who may want to cause you harm is to keep a low profile and take precautions when doing business with the public. You should have tenants mail monthly rental checks to a post office box instead of to your home residence, and you can have an unlisted phone number. Because you own real estate, some people may view you as wealthy target, so be on the lookout for ways to keep a lower profile.

If you want to find out how easily accessible your personal information is, do an internet search for yourself with people-finder companies such as:

privateeye.com
web-detective.com

It's surprising how much of your life is available for anyone to see. Now, all my business and private mail, including rental checks, goes to my P.O. Box. If I have to give a phone number, I give my cell phone. I just purchase minutes when I need them, without a contract, so my number cannot be tracked back to me. If my address is requested on any kind of form, I always give my P.O. Box address. Sage advice comes from J.J. Luna in *How to Be Invisible* who states, "do not, as long as you live, ever again allow your real name to be coupled with your home address."

In his book, Luna relates a story about a former husband who tracked his wife down to her job. The husband killed his wife and several other people who worked at the company. The owner of the company managed to avoid the same fate because he had a P.O. Box listed for a home address. The lesson is, don't make your personal information available to the general public.

9
Let the Tax Law Help You Make Money

There is no security in life. There is only opportunity.

-Douglas MacArthur

The Tax Codes

A chief benefit of real estate investing is tax savings. Deductible expenses include mortgage interest payments, insurance, utilities, cleaning and maintenance services, repairs, advertising costs and management fees, necessary travel expenses as well as depreciation. A good guide to saving money on taxes, without crossing the line into tax evasion, is John T. Reed's *Aggressive Tax Avoidance for Real Estate Investors*.

Having done my best to translate the tax codes, be aware that this information changes each year, and a professional accountant may interpret it differently than I do. While this chapter will be useful as a guide, hire a competent accountant to do your taxes, you'll save time and money. I also recommend that you work out your tax forms prior to shipping them to your accountant, as an exercise in developing expertise in this area.

Some useful IRS publications to refer to are:

Selling your home
http://www.irs.gov/pub/irs-pdf/p523.pdf

Residential Rental Property
http://www.irs.gov/pub/irs-pdf/p527.pdf

Business Expenses
http://www.irs.gov/pub/irs-pdf/p535.pdf

How to Depreciate Property
http://www.irs.gov/pub/irs-pdf/p946.pdf

Repairs vs. Improvements

Although this can be a difficult concept it's well worth the time spent in understanding it. As described in IRS Publication 527, *Residential Rental Property*, you can deduct the cost of repairs to a rental property but you cannot deduct the cost of improvements. You will recover the costs of your improvements when you take depreciation for your property. The difference between the two concepts is easier to grasp when we look at some examples.

Repairs

A repair, as the name implies, fixes something that is broken. It doesn't add to the value of your property or extend its life. Examples of repairs include:

- *inside or outside painting*
- *repairing gutters*
- *fixing floors*
- *fixing leaks*
- *plastering*
- *replacing broken windows*

Improvements

Improvements add to the value of a house prolong its life, or adapts it to new uses. Examples of improvements include adding:

- *a porch, deck, patio, bedroom or bathroom*
- *landscaping, a driveway a fence or a swimming pool*

- *a heating system or air conditioner*
- *a water heater, soft water system or filtration system*
- *flooring, wall-to-wall carpeting of kitchen modernization*
- *insulating attics walls, floor, pipes or ductwork*

Improvement costs are capitalized, meaning that you recover the costs by taking depreciation over time.

Travel Expenses: Let the IRS Help Keep You in Touch with Your Properties

If you use your personal car, pickup truck, or light van for rental activities, such as to collect rental income, to manage, to conserve or to maintain your rental property, you can deduct the expenses. The mileage rate at the time this book is being published is just under 50 cents a mile. You must keep written records of the dates you traveled and the miles you traveled.

Depreciate Property Used in Rental Activities

Depreciation in theory reflects the lowering value of property over time. If you buy furniture for a rental house it will gradually wear out in a few years. The value of furniture can be depreciated, or written off as a deduction on your tax return over a five or a nine-year period, depending upon which method you choose.

In the case of a house or apartment complex, the value of your real estate is considered to go from the purchase price you originally paid to zero over the course of 27½ years. The land that the house sits on does not wear out therefore you are not allowed to depreciate it. Land is usually considered to constitute 20% of the value of a house.

While homes and apartment buildings are considered by the IRS to depreciate in value, in reality they actually increase in value due to inflation, a growing economy or increased demand. Depreciation deductions can be considered as an encouragement from the government to assist those of us who invest in real estate. And this encouragement allows us to shelter otherwise taxable income.

The definition of property that can be depreciated is expanded beyond the house you purchase. "Property", in this case, also includes the following (from the Ernst & Young Tax Guide):

- *Computers and peripheral equipment*
- *Office machinery such as:*
  Typewriters
  Calculators
  Copiers
- *Automobiles*
- *Light trucks*
- *Appliances, including:*
  Stoves
  Ovens
- *Carpets*
- *Furniture used in rental property*
- *Office furniture and equipment, such as:*
  Desks
  Files
- *Roads*
- *Shrubbery*
- *Fences*

Allowable Expense Deductions in Schedule E

Schedule E in tax form 1040 allows the following deductible expenses for your rental properties (Table 9.1).

Table 9.1
Allowable Expense Deductions in Schedule E

1. Advertising.
2. Travel.
3. Mortgage interest.
4. Repairs.
5. Utilities.
6. Property Taxes.
7. Cleaning and maintenance.
8. Management fees.
9. Supplies.
10. Other.
11. Legal and other professional fees.

Below are some of the expenses that I deduct for each category.

1. Advertising. Any money that I spend for classified advertising, signs, magic markers or from printing one-page ads for handing out or posting.

2. Travel. Each time I drive to a rental property I make a note of the mileage traveled. I usually try to drive by each property at least once a week.

3. Mortgage interest. The biggest tax break that you'll receive is for the interest that you pay on your loan. All of the interest is deductible, unless your loan is exceptionally large.

4. Repair. This includes whether I purchase materials for house repairs or if I paid someone to work for me. Tools purchased for use on the property, this includes drills, drill bits, stud finders, levels and saws (in general, any small tools). Books used for fix-up or investing are deductible.

5. Utilities. Each month that I pay water, electricity or gas, between the time when I put the house up for rent and finally rent it out, is deductible. Also, if I pay water (or other utilities) for the property, while it is rented out, that is deductible.

6. Taxes. Property taxes are deductible.

7. Cleaning and maintenance, including carpet cleaning, roof repair, painting and landscaping.

8. Management fees. If I pay a company to find tenants, collect rents and do repairs to the property, I can deduct it.

9. Supplies. The tax code describes deductions as all "ordinary and necessary" expenses to the production of income. The smaller the item (screwdrivers, paint brushes, paint and generally items under about $200 or so), the more likely that it is an expendable supply. Where it gets more uncertain is the "gray area" things - $500 dollar extension ladders and $750 radial arm saws, or things that are not just for the rental properties. Items that are for personal use are non-deductible. The old saying that "pigs get fat; hogs get slaughtered" applies to this category. See your tax advisor to be safe.

10. Other. Additional expenses not covered in other categories.

11. Legal and other professional fees. Tax help is deductible. Purchasing tax books, CD's, or hiring an accountant to do your taxes are all tax deductible.

The Great News about Depreciation, if You Never Sell

The good news about depreciation is that it lowers your present tax bill. The bad news about depreciation is that when you sell an investment property you must pay taxes on the depreciation that you took over the 27½- year life of the property. If you never sell you never pay those taxes.

Keeping Records

It is important for you to keep good records of your real estate transactions. This is valuable not only in case you are audited, but also for the more immediate need of keeping your financial transactions clear in your own mind. If your record keeping is disorganized you can lose a lot of money.

First you must have an accounting notebook where all of your money coming in and going out is noted. I use a 6-column Columnar Pad. I use one column for the date of the transaction, one column for a credit (e.g., rent paid to me), one column for a debit (mortgage that I paid), and one column for notes.

You must keep all receipts if you want to deduct expenses. I have a separate file folder for deduction receipts for each property. I place them in the file as the year goes by. On the back of each receipt I write which property the item was used for and what it was used for. Then at tax time, I type the receipts from each file onto a separate spread sheet on my computer. I turn all of these sheets over to an accountant who does my tax returns. I could, and have done my own taxes. But the advantage of having some one else do your taxes is that it's faster and the charges are tax deductible. In addition, I like to be able to pick up the phone and ask my accountant questions about the tax code throughout the year. In the long run I feel I have saved a lot more money than I have spent by having an accountant.

Keep Personal Account and Business Account Separate

I recommend having a credit card for purchases of repair items for your properties. This gives you another layer of evidence for what you have purchased. It also helps to remind you of potential deductions in case you misplace receipts.

It's also a good idea to establish a separate checking account to use for rental payments and for security deposits. It makes everything you do less confusing if you separate your personal account from your business. I don't recommend getting a business account for your properties. Banks usually charge monthly fees for a business account, but there is no need to pay this additional expense. What I did was to start a regular checking account in a different bank from where I have my personal checking. A separate bank allows me to keep things straight in my mind and there is no charge for a regular account, except to order checks.

10

Make Work a Family Affair

The greatest gift that you can give your child is the strength to solve his own problems.

-Melissa & Harry H. Harrison, Jr.

Bite Size Pieces for Small Fries

For the first fix-up house that my wife and I bought, our two boys were 4 and 7 years old. Some people might think that they couldn't do much at that age. My experience is that children can learn lot, and sometimes help you in the process, if you adjust the work to their level and let them do what is interesting to them. At that age they like to try out as many different activities as they can. My philosophy is let them hammer some nails, even if they bend them. Let them paint even if they spill a few drops (or buckets). Usually the paint ends up on their clothes, the ground, or sometimes the dog. One time, I took a picture of my kids painting a fence because they actually got some paint on the fence!

Let them cut tree branches even if the branches that they can cut are no bigger than a twig. In other words, include them in any activity that they want to be included in. They are learning. If they make mistakes, take it lightly and laugh a lot. Keep them interested by giving them a lot of different jobs to do. Make them feel good about themselves. In the long run, that's more important than all the fix-up houses in the world.

Some activities which my children participated in:

-picking up nails
-sweeping
-small paint jobs
-putting landscaping rocks in wheelbarrows
-digging holes for plants
-watering plants
-removing old nails from boards (with supervision)

One activity that our 7-year-old undertook amazed me by his creativity and insight into the building process. He took scraps of wood, some cardboard, and bits and pieces of discarded items, and he constructed a play house. Give kids some tools and a little freedom and their creativity is astounding.

Another advantage of having the kids with you on the job is that they get to see first hand how my wife and I interact while we work together. They see that we respect each other and help each other. The family that *works* and plays together stays together.

It's also important for kids to have down time where they do things unrelated to the fix-up activities. Take them to garage sales and buy them toys, go to parks and play with them till they drop or take them to movies. Almost every evening after working on our first fix-up property we would walk, or skateboard, to a nearby park and let the kids play for as long as they wanted to. Balance out the work and play.

Hire Your Kids and Add Tax Breaks

At first, we paid our kids $1 a day for each day that they did some work on the fix-up house, and we were pretty lenient as to what constituted "work". But they learned a little about the value of work, completing a task, and making money by turning something of little value into something useful. Now, our kids are older and we pay them by the hour for the work they do.

As kids get older, there are tax benefits to putting them to work for you. These include:

1. Your children will probably not pay taxes. Each child can earn around $4,000 a year without being subject to any federal income tax.

2. You get to deduct the wages. As long as the amounts paid are a legitimate business expense, you can deduct them from your taxable enterprise income. This can be a big tax savings. For example, if you're in the 28% tax bracket and pay your child $3,000 that otherwise would be income for yourself, you'll save $810 in taxes. That's better than giving your child the money for doing nothing, and getting no deduction in return.

3. You increase your other tax breaks. The amount that you pay your kids reduces your adjusted gross income. This may qualify you for some of the tax deductions and credits that are not available to taxpayers with higher incomes.

11

A Tale of Two Investment Strategies: Avenida Planeta and Calle Canis

Opportunity is missed by most people because it is dressed in overalls and looks like work.

-Thomas Edison

This chapter examines two houses that I have purchased and the two different investment strategies that I utilize. Each strategy is broken down into how I found and acquired the property, an analysis of the house, what was repaired and its rental history.

Strategy 1: The Planeta House: Buy and Hold

This is an example of the buy and hold strategy. My wife and I bought this house and held onto it to make money from rents and through appreciation.

<u>Finding the property</u>

I came across this property in the newspaper want ads. The ad read:

> Fix-up house for sale. Repossessed by bank. Will take best offer. Open 9-4:00 Sat. & Sun. 1709 S. Avenida Planeta. Reality Executives 661-3609.

I drove over to see the property. It was not in my target area, but it was in a nice neighborhood. The houses in the neighborhood were well kept. This case shows that you need to be flexible when investing in real estate. You must take advantage of great deals that may appear out of nowhere, or in this case, outside my target area.

I called up my friend/handyman who works with me and we went over and inspected the house. The house looked pretty bad. Some of the required repairs included:

-the back fence and front fences had been knocked down and cars had driven around in the back yard.

-all of the back windows had been broken.
-it hadn't been painted in decades, inside or out.
-the kitchen needed a new stove.
-many of the inside doors had holes in the (typical of a repossessed house).
-bathroom sinks, toilets and one shower stall had to be replaced.

It looked pretty bad but there was no structural damage. On the positive side the house had:

-a huge back yard.
-a nice single-car carport and adjoining storage shed.
-a large back porch.
-solid brick construction.

Analysis of the House

While there was a lot of damage, I knew that I could fix most of it up without too much trouble. The realtor said the bank wanted around $85,000 and was taking bids. I did a check and found that other houses in the area had been selling for $110,000-115,000, so there was $25,000-30,000 in equity in it. I offered $85,500 and my bid was selected. I'm sure that other bidders thought the place was trashed out enough that a lower bid would be accepted. My philosophy is that if it's a good house that I know I want, I bid higher than the minimum, so that I am more likely to be selected. Why lose a good property by trying to save a relatively few bucks? In the long run you lose tens, or hundreds of thousands of dollars. I took out a standard 30-year loan at 7.5% interest from a mortgage company (Table 11.1).

Table 11.1 Planeta House Numbers	
Purchase Price	$85,500
Improved value	$110-115,000
Equity after improvements	$25,000-30,000
Interest rate	7.5% originally, then re-financed for 6.1%
Monthly mortgage payments	$703
Rent received	$800 initially/now $875
Present Value	$185,000

Fix up

I was working full-time at my day job, so I did the fix-up work on weekends and evenings. The first thing I did was to establish control of the back yard. Even before I took possession of the back yard, as the paperwork was grinding its way through the approval process, I put up a 5 foot plastic fence where the back fence used to be, to keep people and cars out of the property. As soon as I took possession, I put up a secure wooden fence in the back, and on the sides of the house. Security was my first concern. To replace the broken windows, I made 7 calls until a found what I considered a fair bid to replace the broken windows. I found an independent window repair man who could undercut the prices of the larger companies. It almost always pays to make lots of calls before contracting out a job. From there it was just painting and repairing. I bought a stove top from a friend to replace the broken one. I replaced many of the outdated switches and outlets, and I put roof coating on the flat roof. In all, it took about 3 months to fix-up the house.

Rent

The house rented out for $800 /mo. A tenant stayed for four years, after which I raised the rent to $875. Rents in neighborhood rental properties had been rising over the 4 years that my house had been rented out. I usually wait to raise rents until a tenant leaves and a new one goes in. I was paying $703 mortgage payments (Table 11.1).

Appreciation

The house appreciated from its original value of $110,000 (after fix-up) to $185,000, four years later. That period was an economic boom time for real estate investors, and prices shot up like a rocket. My plan was to keep this house as a rental house. The house is in a good location and fairly easy to rent. It brings in a good monthly rent that will go up over time.

Strategy 2: The Canis House: Buy, Live In, and Sell with No Tax Liability

My wife and I bought this house with the intention of fixing it up, living in it for two or three years, and then selling it. We thought that the combination of adding value to the house through fixing it up, and the increase in equity over two years, would give us a pot of money at the end to buy more properties.

Finding the property

This house was a repossessed Veterans Administration house. I found it advertised on the VA web page and drove over to visit it during an open house. The Canis house was in the same neighborhood as the Planeta house, so I knew it was a good area. It was definitely a fix-up house, in some ways in need of more repair work than the Planeta House.

Some of the fix-up work needed at the Canis house included:

-new walls and ceilings in both bedrooms (damaged by a leaking cooler unit on the roof).
-floor tile needed in some rooms of house.
-new cooler on roof.
-toilets and vanities needed in bathrooms.
-painting inside and out.
-landscaping in front and back yards.

Positive aspects of the house included:

-a large two-car carport.
-big back yard.
-swimming pool (which needed a pump).
-a fairly large house (1600 sq. ft).
-great floor tile in most of the house.

Analysis of the house

The house was in a nice neighborhood, but it was located close to a main street, so there was some noise from the street. Landscaping and walls reduced the noise from cars but not completely. This was one reason that we thought this house might work better as a house to sell, instead of keeping it as a rental.

Living in the house and repairing it gradually, helps to overcome the problem of paying the mortgage when you aren't making any money from tenants. It's a big drain on your budget until you can move someone into the house. By living in the house, you avoid that problem, although you face the problem of inconvenience, i.e., of living in a house that is more of a work area than a house. But, in reality, that is only a minor problem. It is easily overcome with a positive attitude, a sense of adventure and by fixing vital areas of the house first, like the bathroom and the kitchen.

The minimum bid was $100,000 and I submitted a bid of $104,000 (Table 11.2), utilizing my same philosophy of trying to slightly outbid everyone else. The house was in a nicer area of the neighborhood than the Planeta house and houses in the area at that time were selling for $130,000.

Table 11.2 Canis House Numbers	
Purchase price	$104,000
Improved value	$130,000
Equity after improvements	$26,000
Interest rate	5.875%
Mortgage payments	764/mo.
Present value	$220,000

Fix up

It was nice not to have to travel across town to do repairs on a fix-up house, and to have all my tools at hand. On the negative side, repairs went in spurts without the strong financial motivation to repair the house as quickly as possible.

The handyman helped me install the new cooler. My brother and I installed tiles in one bathroom, and my wife and

I installed floor tiles in one bedroom and other smaller areas that were not completed by the previous owners.

My wife and I got up early in the mornings, before our kids were up, to work on the landscaping for the huge front and backyards. We bought tile and composite wood flooring when it was on sale. We bought a used kitchen cabinet set at one of the construction material recycle stores for $400, a fraction of what we would have had to pay new. Habitat for Humanity operates one of the stores in our town. Another is operated by a Tucson philanthropic group that uses the profits to assist needy families. Habitat for Humanity is a national group that builds houses for people who lack the resources to have a house otherwise. We have saved thousands of dollars in these stores. Construction companies donate surplus building materials to the stores and the proceeds go to the charitable work of the group. To find a Habitat store in your area check the Habitat website at:

http://www.habitat.org/env/restore.aspx.

Appreciation and sale

The Canis house appreciated in value from our purchase price of $104,000 to $220,000. As with the Planeta house, it was a time of wild appreciation in the housing market. We soon plan to sell the Canis house for $220,000. We refinanced the house and took out about $20,000, leaving us with a $120,000 mortgage. We are selling the property ourselves, paying no taxes since we lived in the house for over two years. We will use the approximate $100,000 equity as down payment to buy to purchase our next fix-up property.

The 3-House Solution

One way that to manage your real estate business so that it fits in with your day job and family commitments is by combing the buy-and-hold strategy with the buy-live in-and-sell strategy. I call this the 3-House Solution for the real estate investor with a busy life. It is a way to minimize the time spent managing properties, and maximize equity growth. The approach consists of two simple steps:

Step 1.) Buy 2 houses that you fix-up and rent out. These are houses that are in areas of town where the demand for rentals is high, and can be rented out fairly easily. In my case, the only advertising that I usually do is to put a "For Rent" sign in the window. By keeping a maximum of two rental properties, it keeps your management burden at reasonable levels. If you have a partner who doesn't have a full-time job, you may be able to handle more than two rentals.

Step 2.) Buy a third house that you live in as you repair it, with the idea to sell it in 2 to 5 years. This house should be in a stable residential area where most of the homes are owner-occupied, and there are few rentals. After you have lived in the house for at least two years and fixed it up, you sell it utilizing the 1997 Taxpayer Relief Act exemption to pay no federal taxes on the sale. After you sell, you buy a bigger and better house.

Under the 3-House Solution, the two rental houses bring in a steadily increasing monthly rental income. Managing two properties does not interfere with your 9-5:00 job. The rents will be a small amount at the beginning, but grow over time. Each time you put a new tenant into one of the houses, you raise the rent from what the previous tenant paid. Once the mortgages are paid off, then the monthly income becomes sizable.

The third house, which you fix up to sell, allows you to build up larger equity each time you turn it over. The nice thing about the third house is that you build up your equity on weekends or evenings, as you repair the house, and since you live in the house, it eliminates the responsi - bility to deal with too many tenants.

12

The Big Picture: Even When You Lose You Win

Get a few good laughs and do the best you can. Live your life so that even when you lose you win.

-Will Rogers

To see the big picture, we must look beyond the physical aspects of buying, fixing-up and renting houses. One aspect of the big picture is that you don't take life too seriously, enjoy the little things, and spend time with your spouse and children. When you meet a setback, take it for what it is, a chance to learn something and do better next time. Without setbacks we would never grow.

Sure we want to make money to provide for our families and by making money we can do more to help others. The rising tide raises all boats. But take time for early morning walks to watch the sun come up and evening walks with the family and pet dog to enjoy the cool air and family time together. In life, we never know how much time we have left to do some of our most cherished activities or to be with our family and close friends. As we get older, we ask ourselves "How many more times will I see the sun set behind the mountains," or "How many times will I be able to share laughter with a good friend" or hike one of my favorite mountain trails or read books to the kids before they go to sleep. A hundred times? Ten times? Five times, or only one more time? It is the uncertainty that makes us appreciate these things all the more.

Teach What You Have Learned

A second aspect of the big picture is to see that buying and fixing up houses is only the first step in the process. After you've done it for a few years, and start to master all aspects of your chosen fix-up profession, it is time to move on to teaching others how to do it.

Keep notes and lots of pictures of your fix-up properties, with before and after photos. You will need them later for teaching.

Have a file section for each house in your file cabinet with application & closing documents, copies of rental checks received. Get into the habit of documenting everything you do.

Go to Toastmasters to practice public speaking and general interpersonal communication skills. It's a great place to practice talking about what you do with fix-up houses and a unbeatable source of good jokes. Toastmasters is where you can hone your skills.

Teach a class at the community college or at an open university, on what you have learned in real estate. You will learn a lot more than you might expect by preparing for the classes. It will fill in a lot of gaps in your own knowledge. If you really want to learn something, you teach it. There are three steps to knowledge:

1) study
2) do
3) teach.

Tape your classroom presentations on sound tapes or video tapes, for your own review and for future use.

Write a Book

If you really want to learn something, write a book about it. Writing forces you to study a topic intensely so that you understand so completely that you can explain it to someone else. The chapter on taxes in this book was a big challenge to me. I thought I knew about taxes, but once I tried to put what I knew on paper, I realized that I didn't know it well enough to explain it. I had to do my research. You have to immerse yourself in the topic. Your mind must be so full of information that it overflows onto the page.

An old Chinese proverb says that before you die, you must to three things: plant a tree, have a child and write a book. This book started as just a dream that would not go away. I knew it would take a lot of work to write a book about my real estate experiences, but it was an idea that was stuck in the back of my mind, like bubble gum in hair.

Finally, I sat down at the computer and started hammering it out. I worked late at night and early in the mornings when everyone else was asleep. I started writing in the spring and set a goal to finish by my birthday, August 12th. (Fortunately, I didn't specify a year because here I am three years later still writing.) I tried to crank out two pages a day. Before I knew it I was too far along to turn back. I knew that I wasn't a great writer, but I took heart author Robert Benchley's comment, "It took me fifteen years to discover I had no talent for writing, but I couldn't give it up because by that time, I was too famous."

As you write a book you become an information magnet and tidbit junkie. I was tuned into all kinds of information related to my topic. I commonly spotted good articles in newspapers, magazines and on the computer that addressed topics that I wanted to cover in the book. I also was tuned into taking classes or seminars that would advance my knowledge. And, whenever an opportunity presented itself, or often even if it didn't present itself, I would ask people with specialized knowledge, like lawyers and accountants, to clear up gray areas in my understanding.

It's amazing how the mind works. You plant a seed in your mind by reading about something that deep inside yourself you know you would like to do, like write a book. And even though you stop thinking about it consciously, sub-consciously your mind keeps thinking about it. Your mind starts developing ways to make the dream a reality. Eventually, you start to think, "I could probably do that, but I don't have time." Then your mind comes back a few days or weeks later with the thought, "But you could carry a note book with you everywhere you go and jot down ideas while waiting for a bus or at lunchtime, or instead of watching television." Then you think, "But a publishing company would never publish my book." Your mind comes back again with the thought, "You could study and learn how to publish your own book." And so it goes, for each obstacle you come up with your mind comes up with a solution, until you reach the point where you say to yourself, "I'm going to do it, no matter what it takes".

Write a book. Become an expert. An expert is just a normal person who has written a book. Who better can describe the things you know and have learned than yourself? You might fail in your attempt, but you just might succeed beyond your dreams.

A New Beginning: Write Your Own Ending

Well known television and movie personality, Kermit the Frog, once said, "Life is like a movie, you can write your own ending." Now you know what I have learned. You can buy low-priced fix-up houses, and gradually build your knowledge and wealth. You can make money monthly by renting out your properties. By re-financing, you can take equity out of your properties to purchase more houses, or sell houses and pay no federal tax. You will save money by deducting expenses and make money on appreciation. You will be less and less reliant on your present job to make ends meet. Don't be afraid to make mistakes. Remember, even if you lose, you win. I made it work, and it continues to bring me short-term and long-term profits, so I know that you can do it too.

Before you know it, you'll be ready to write your own fix-up story. Don't forget to send me a copy when you finish.

References

Adams, Douglas, 1979, The *Hitchhiker's Guide to the Galaxy*, New York: Random House.

Bradbury, Ray, 1992, *Zen and the Art of Writing*, New York: Bantam Books.

Bernstein, Peter W., editor, *The Ernst and Young Tax Guide 2005*, Hoboken: John Wiley & Sons, Inc.

Brangham, Suzanne, 1987, *Housewise*, New York: Clarkson N. Potter, Inc.

Casler, Carlton, 2002, *Arizona Landlord's Deskbook*, Phoenix: The Consumer Law Books Publishing House.

DeCima, Jay P., 2003, *Investing in Fixer-Uppers*, New York: McGraw-Hill.

Dexter, Steve, 2007, *Real Estate Debt Can Make Your Rich*, New York: McGraw-Hill.

Dominguez, Joe and Vicki Robin, 1992, *Your Money or Your Life*, New York: Penguin Books.

Dworin, Lawrence, 1990, *Profits in Buying & Renovating Homes*, Carlsbad: Craftsman Book Company.

Edwards, Paul and Sarah, 1991, *Making it on Your Own*, New York: Jeremy P. Tarcher/Perigee Books.

Eldred, Gary, 2003, *The 106 Common Mistakes Homebuyers Make (and How to Avoid Them),* Hoboken: John Wiley & Sons.

Harrison, Melissa and Harry H. Harrison, Jr., 2006, *Mother to Son,* New York: Workman Publishing Company.

Herbert, Frank, 1965, *Dune,* Chilton Books.

Kristof, Kathy, 2006, Many Factors go into Calculating Credit Score, *Arizona Daily Star,* March 26, p. D2.

Luna, J.J., 2004, *How to be Invisible,* New York: Thomas Dunne Books.

Milin, Irene and Mike, 1988, *How to Buy & Manage Rental Properties,* New York: Simon & Schuster.

McLean, Andrew and Gary W. Eldred, 2003, *Investing in Real Estate,* New York: John Wiley & Sons.

Nickerson, William, 1969, *How I Turned $1,000 into Three Million in Real Estate – In My Spare Time,* New York: Simon and Schuster.

Reed, John T., 1996, *Aggressive Tax Avoidance for Real Estate Investors.* Danville: John T. Reed Publishing.

Schaub, John W., 2005, *Building Wealth One House at a Time,* New York: McGraw-Hill.

Sinetar, Marsha, 1987, *Do What You Love and the Money Will Follow,* New York: Dell Publishing.

Sinetar, Marsha, 1995, *To Build the Life You Want, Create the Work You Love*, New York: St. Martin's Press.

Tzu, Lao, *The Way of Life*.

United States Census Bureau, 2006, http://www.census.gov/.

Thoreau, Henry D., 2004, *Walden*, Princeton: Princeton University Press.

Weir, Mary, House *Recycling, The Best Real Estate Opportunity for the '80s*, Chicago: Contemporary Books, Inc.

Appendices

Appendix A
The Compressed Version of
How to Buy, Repair and Rent Out Your
First Fix-up House

1. Determine what you really value in life.
2. Get your financial house in order.
   Check your credit scores and repair them if necessary.
3. Study and develop skills.
   Accumulate useful books.
   Take classes in electrical wiring, plumbing, etc. at community college.
   Attend seminars and classes on real estate investing.
   Scan newspapers for potential fix-up properties.
   Check HUD and VA websites or pickup printed lists from realtors.
   Drive through target areas.
4. Pre-qualify for a loan.
5. Locate property that is priced below market, neighboring houses are selling for 10-20% less.
   Inspect the house carefully, with an experienced handyman or inspector, if necessary.
   Estimate fix-up costs and monthly loan payments, determine if it will be profitable.
   If it's a VA of HUD house, work with a realtor to make a bid.
6. Purchase property.
7. Fix-up the property.
   Read "The Way of Life" to get deeper view of repairing houses and learn how to appreciate the invisible forces of nature.
   Do as much as you can by yourself, learn as you go.

Hire out complicated repairs, but observe how they are done.

8. Put out "for rent" sign.

Hold open houses on weekends.

Have interested persons fill out applications and chat them up to find out more information about them.

Check out references, criminal background and credit for best applicants.

Fill out contract with tenants, tenants fill out home inspection form.

Give tenants copy of lead paint pamphlet if house built before 1977.

Collect damage deposit and first month's rent.

9. Manage money.

Have rents paid to your P.O. Box & receive calls only on cell phone.

Set up a separate bank account to deposit rent and damage deposit.

Keep good records.

10. Teach what you have learned.

Appendix B
Useful Websites

**Fixer Uppers and Rental Houses Blog
(my blog)**
www.fixemup.org

Habitat for Humanity Re-Store Locations
http://www.habitat.org/env/restore.aspx

Home Values
http://www.zillow.com/

Housing and Urban Development (HUD) and Veterans Administration (VA) Repossessed Properties
This site also has links to houses from other federal agencies, including VA houses.
http://www.hud.gov/homes/homesforsale.cfm

Internal Revenue Service
Selling your home, http://www.irs.gov/pub/irs-pdf/p523.pdf
Residential Rental Property, http://www.irs.gov/pub/irs-pdf/p527.pdf
Business Expenses, http://www.irs.gov/pub/irs-pdf/p535.pdf
How to Depreciate Property, http://www.irs.gov/pub/irs-pdf/p946.pdf

Landlording/Background Checks
MrLandlord.com

Mortgage Rate Calculator
http://list.realestate.yahoo.com/re/calculators/payment.ht
ml

Parcel Information Search
To search for background and historical information on
property in Pima County, Arizona. Other counties provide
similar information.
http://www.dot.co.pima.az.us/gis/maps/landbase/parsrch.
htm

Pima Courts of Justice
To do background checks on potential tenants. Other counties provide similar information.
http://geronimo.jp.co.pima.az.us/casesearch/

Appendix C
Recommended Reference Materials

Fix-up Books (in order of frequency that I use them)

New Complete Guide to Home Repair & Improvement by Better Homes and Gardens.

A book that is useful because it covers an extremely broad variety of subjects. You can find almost any home repair project in this book. In some cases you must get a more specialized book for more in-depth information, but this book gets you started.

Fix-it-Yourself Manual by Readers Digest.

Another very useful book that gives you good instruction on doing repairs around the house.

The Complete Fix-It-Yourself Manuel by Time Life Books

A great book for repairing broken appliances. There is none better. Great pictures, easy to follow instructions. You can repair appliances like a pro without actually being one.

Profits in Buying & Renovating Homes by Lawrence Dworin.

Another great book for aspiring repair pros. The author goes into great detail, with before and after pictures, on what to repair in your fix-up house and how to do it cheaply.

Wiring 1-2-3: Install, Upgrade, Repair, and Maintain Your Home's Electrical System by The Home Depot.

A good book that tells you step-by-step to do a variety of common upgrades and repairs to a home electrical system.

The Complete Guide to Home Wiring: A Comprehensive Manual from Basic Repairs to Advanced Projects by Black & Decker.

Similar to the previous one but it takes you a step further to more advanced electrical projects.

Kitchen and Bathroom Plumbing by Time Life Books.

Plumbing 1-2-3 by The Home Depot.

Flooring 1-2-3 by The Home Depot.

Motivation/Inspiration Materials

Abraham Lincoln, a book by Carl Sandburg.

The Way of Life, by Lao Tzu.

Regarding Henry, a movie starring Harrison Ford.

Appendix D
Credit Reports

To get a copy of your own credit report you can contact the following three main credit reporting agencies.

Equifax
Provides your FICO score and one credit bureau report, www.equifax.com or (1-800-685-1111)

Experian
Utilizes the Fair Isaac credit-score, www.experian.com or (1-888-397-3742)

TransUnion
FICO score and one credit bureau score, www.transunion.com or (1-800-888-4213)

Index

LaVergne, TN USA
14 October 2009
160830LV00003B/106/P

9 780979 856617